If Rednecks
HAD BEEN THE
CHOSEN PEOPLE

Charlie Thompson

D0684281

RUTLEDGE HILL PRESS®

Nashville, Tennessee

Published in Nashville, Tennessee, by Rutledge Hill Press®, 211 Seventh Avenue North, Nashville, Tennessee 37219.

Distributed in Canada by H. B. Fenn & Company, Ltd., 34 Nixon Road, Bolton, Ontario L7E 1W2.
Distributed in Australia by The Five Mile Press Pty., Ltd., 22 Summit Road, Noble Park, Victoria 3174.
Distributed in New Zealand by Southern Publishers Group, 22 Burleigh Street, Grafton, Auckland, New Zealand.
Distributed in the United Kingdom by Verulam Publishing, Ltd., 152a Park Street Lane, Park Street, St. Albans, Hertfordshire AL2 2AU.

Typography by E.T. Lowe, Nashville, Tennessee

Design and illustrations by Robert Schwalb

Library of Congress Cataloging-in-Publication Data

Thompson, Charlie, 1946-
    If rednecks had been the chosen people / Charlie Thompson.
    p. cm.
    ISBN 1-55853-743-0 (pbk.)
    1. Bible. O.T.—Humor. I. Title.
    PN6231.B45T48 1999   98-49763
    220.9'505'0207—dc21   CIP

Printed in the United States of America

1 2 3 4 5 6 7 8 9—02 01 00 99

CONTENTS

To Lucy and Holly, my chosen people

. . . God has chosen you to be a people for Himself,
a special treasure above all the peoples on the face of the earth.
Deuteronomy 7:6 (NKJ)

INTRODUCTION

Being a die-hard Southerner can have a profound effect on the way you look at the world around you—even the Bible. We refer to the South as the "Bible Belt" and "God's Country." We continually give thanks for being "Southern by the grace of God". Why then is there no mention of us, the descendants of Bubba, in the scriptures?

It occurred to me that if Columbus had sailed a few thousand years earlier, Southerners most likely would have been God's Chosen People. The main story line and principles would have remained the same, but good ol' boys would have been a whole lot more fun to watch. God might have created "Adam Bob" because He wanted a fishing buddy. "Noah Bob" probably would have had more trouble getting his wife's luggage on the ark than he had loading the animals. "Moose" might have needed a few more than ten commandments to keep that rowdy bunch in line. And you can just bet the Promised Land would have been located right smack dab in the Heart of Dixie . . . if Rednecks had been the Chosen People.

This book is not a theological treatise of alternative interpretations of poignant scriptural paragons. (Whatever that means; I ain't that smart.) But neither is this book intended to be sacrilegious or irreverent. I am that smart. The RNV (Redneck Version) is simply my way of looking at some familiar old Bible stories from a slightly different and somewhat humorous angle.

So grab a big ol' glass of sweet tea, sit back, and enjoy finding yourself, or at least some of your close kin, wandering through these pages.

P. S. For additional reading, I would highly recommend the original Book. It's a whole lot more interesting and inspiring.

If Rednecks

HAD BEEN THE

CHOSEN PEOPLE

I Should Never
Have Made That Snake

n the beginning, God created Alabama. He saw that it was good and spent the rest of the week bream fishing on the Tombigbee River.

Fishing was good and, naturally, He caught the limit every day. But fishing just isn't as much fun alone. He didn't have anybody to help with the anchors or run the trolling motor. It's no fun to laugh at yourself when you cast into the top of a tree and you need someone to share the melodious echo of a riverbank belch. God needed a fishing buddy. So from the mud of the bank, He made Adam Bob in His own image. Well, not exactly. Adam Bob had this good-sized gap between his front teeth and ears that could double as satellite dishes, but other than that, close.

God was happy with His new creation and decided to let Adam Bob name all the creatures around them. Once God convinced him that He didn't mean names like Shorty, Stinky, and Leon, Adam Bob caught on and names like possum, bluegill, jaybird, etc., started rolling off his tongue. He even came up with cottonmouth water moccasin after God got him to come down out of the tree. Part of that deal was that God had to pull the legs off that thing so that Adam Bob could out-run it.

Everything seemed to be going pretty well, except that God began to notice that Adam Bob occasion-ally had a kinda "hang-dog" look on his face. While naming the ani-mals, Adam Bob had become aware that for every Bobby Bunny, there was a Betty Bunny; for every Tommy Turtle, there was a Tammy Turtle; for every Sammy Snake, there was . . .

well, that was hard to tell, and Adam Bob wasn't going to get that close. Nevertheless, there wasn't a Bob-bette for Adam Bob.

So God told Adam Bob that He could make him a companion, but it would cost a rib. Now Adam Bob had been alone for several thousand years, or several minutes—time blurs in a lonely man's mind—and he figured a woman for a rib was a pretty good deal. Matter of fact, he was negotiating to trade both little toes for another one when God told him that one woman was all he needed and more than he could handle. So God made Eveleen.

Now Eveleen was the most gor-geous woman that Adam Bob had ever seen. (Being the only one probably didn't hurt either, what with her wandering left eye and that patch of hair on her back.) Adam Bob was one happy country boy. He finally had somebody to sit close to him in the wagon and watch monkey rasslin on Saturday night. And she smelled a lot better than either one of the dogs.

Life was good—fishing all day with God and Eveleen to come home to at night. She still wouldn't clean fish, but she could fry some great chicken and made the best cornbread in the county. They had their own double-wide cave, a paid-for dug-out bass boat canoe with inboard/outboard paddles, his and her vine swings, and matching fig leaf bowling shirts. Besides that, they could do whatever they wanted, whenever they wanted, and wherever they wanted with virtually no rules. Well, there was that little thing about staying out of the asparagus patch; they could eat anything in the garden except the asparagus. But that was no problem because God knew that nobody in their right mind wanted asparagus anyway.

It was about this time that Eveleen became health conscious. She decided to cut out fatty fried foods and increase fiber in their diet. The aforementioned cotton-mouth snake individual, irritated by the constant stomach rash from having to lie in the mud, had not forgotten that Adam Bob cost him his legs and saw this as an opportunity to get even. Dressing up like Marcus Welby, M.D., he eased up next to Eveleen in the collard patch and introduced himself as a dietary expert. He really didn't look that much like Marcus Welby, but what with Eveleen's left eye pointing somewhere in the direction of where Cleveland might someday be located, he was close enough. He persuaded Eveleen that asparagus was the answer to all their choles-terol and regularity problems. He not only convinced her to pick a mess, but also gave her his special hollandaise recipe. He even implied that it just might inhibit the growth of that hair on her back. That night at supper, Eveleen made Adam Bob close his eyes and open his mouth because she had a surprise for him. After Adam Bob blew the first two mouthfuls into the polyester curtains, Eveleen held his nose until he finally swallowed a couple of stalks. Adam Bob immediately had a bad feeling about what had just happened. This feeling was further confirmed as he spent most of the rest of the night reading the Sears catalog by flashlight in that little house away from the house. That hollandaise can really move a man.

The next morning God was sitting in the boat waiting for Adam Bob. When he finally arrived, instead of his usual overalls, Adam Bob had on a three-piece yuppie suit. "Why in the world are you dressed like that?" God asked (like He didn't already know). "And more importantly, why are you late? The angels got all the best fishing spots."

Being the man that he was, Adam Bob stood straight and tall and confessed, "Everything was that durn snake and Eveleen's fault. How about taking my two little toes and make another woman? Maybe this one will come out with straight eyes and a little less hair this time." God was not amused and told Adam Bob that since he and Eveleen couldn't even keep just one simple rule, they would have to leave Alabama and move to Atlanta to get work. Of course, this also meant that God would have to make Georgia.

While He was making Georgia, it occurred to Him that the SEC really needed more than just Auburn, Alabama, and Georgia (see, He already knew that one day Georgia Tech would defect to the ACC). So He went ahead and made South Carolina, Florida, Mississippi, Louisiana, and Tennessee. This alignment was pleasing to God, especially since more teams created more and bigger rivalries and provided Vanderbilt for homecoming games. He set as emperor of the SEC the formidable Bearius Bryantus, who ruled virtually unchallenged for many seasons.

All the new states provided their own individual charm and areas of interest. Tennessee had scenic mountain vistas from which emanated a series of strange twanging noises that later became known as country music. Mississippi was famous for its Old Man River, which was not only a song but also an actual body of water large enough to float large gambling casinos known as riverboats. Louisiana became famous for lying dormant for many centuries until it was finally purchased from the French (a future creation of unwashed, arrogant people who wear funny hats and live on sauces) by one of our later presidents. Likewise, South Carolina did little to gain public attention until the mid-nineteenth century when a little skirmish at a place called Fort Sumter led to several years of unpleasantness.

Conversely, Florida experienced immediate popularity as a place for visitors from neighboring states to severely charbroil their otherwise lily-white bodies. It also proved an ideal location to house large, silly rodents (Disney World) and stage fantastic fireworks displays (Cape Canaveral). But Florida soon began to fill up with strange and exotic creatures known as (no, not alligators) Yankees (Snowus Birdus).

This brought up another problem. Snow Birds are indigenous to northern states until time for retirement when they migrate immediately to Tampa-Saint Petersburg. Now, much to God's dismay, and totally out of step with the original plan, He had to create the North. But to ensure that they would not become confused with Southerners, He made Yankees talk funny and decreed that while in Florida they must wear Bermuda shorts, dark socks, and sandals.

Then while His creation tools were handy, He went ahead and made Canada 'cause even Yankees deserve to be south of something. Mexico was next, so that Texans didn't look stupid going around hollering "Remember the Alamo" when, without the Mexicans, there wouldn't be anything to remember. California was created because He knew there would eventually be a race of people known as the Dudes, and they needed a place to gather.

Anyway, Adam Bob and Eveleen moved off to Atlanta to fend—shop, get your hair done, take in a ball game—for themselves in an unfamiliar and hostile land. Over the next few weeks they proceeded to have several thousand children, including the brothers, Can't and Able. Can't never could, and this naturally led to some amount of tension because his brother was always Able. One day in a fit of anger, and what witnesses described as a really ugly pale blue leisure suit, Can't backed his eighteen-wheeler over Able (a very difficult task because trucks had not yet been invented and he had to roll the wheels over Able one at a time). As this was the first recorded homicide, Atlanta immediately became the murder capital of the world (FBI Crime Watch Statistics, 5673 B.C. section 1, page 1, paragraph 1—serious crimes: Atlanta 1).

Fortunately for Can't, his court-appointed attorney was successful in challenging all prospective jurors on the grounds that everybody in the world was kin to his client. Even if he had been convicted, his chances for surviving the electric chair were pretty good since electricity had not yet been invented. Electrocution, in those days, was accomplished by having several people shuffle across the carpet during cold weather and touch the condemned on the nose. Although this process could become somewhat annoying after a period of time, it seldom proved fatal. God, not being bound by such earthly jurisprudence, gave Can't a scathing letter of reprimand and banished him to the hinterlands (later renamed New Jersey).

At this time, the action slows down while a lot of begotting happened. Begot is a Greek word meaning *to multiply like congressional committees.* Remember, there weren't a whole lot of folks in the world, and if this homicide thing catches on, there weren't going to be a whole lot more. Adam Bob and Eveleen both lived to ripe old ages of eight hundred or nine hundred years and, as one might expect, were really wrinkled by the time they died.

CHAPTER II

Begotting Can Cause Blindness

egotting became a very popular pastime. This was very good in one sense, because the world really needed more people. But, as is prone (one of the favorite positions for begotting) to happen, people soon began to use begotting not just for procreation but for recreation and entertainment purposes. And worse yet, they be got to forgetting with whom they be supposed to be begotting (do not try this sentence at home unless under the direct supervision of an English major dropout). When they finished begotting at their house, they would continue at the neighbor's house, a friend's house, the White House, the brown house, and sometimes totally by accident, wind up back at their own house. They spent late nights at the local honky-tonk line dancing, pouring Jim Beam down their throats, and stuffing sacks of quarters into the jukebox. After enough Jim Beam, they were making commitments of eternal love to everything from Waffle House waitresses to shrubbery, which, when viewed in a drunken stupor, really does resemble Dolly Parton (the shrubbery, not the waitresses). People were living like current day soap operas, except the acting was much better and there were fewer commercials for medications guaranteed to control yeast infections (caused by prolonged sitting in vats of warm beer). To make matters worse, they were eating asparagus like hotcakes—with butter, syrup, and a side of bacon.

Once again, man had taken what was supposed to be a good thing and turned it into something vile, squalid, depraved, and tailor-made for prime time television. Again, God was not amused. The entirety of His creation had gone bonkers. He was so busy writing up pink slips for transgressions that there was no time left for fishing. Maybe man was not such a good idea after all. In His continued tinkering with this new universe, He had recently come up with an invention that might solve the problem—rain.

Being fair-minded, He decided to look around one more time to see if He could find at least one good ol' boy with whom He might continue this experiment. He looked high and low and was just fixin' to turn on the faucet when south of Montgomery He spotted His man.

Out in the field stood Noah Bob, checking his turnip patch for stink bugs and wearing a pair of snakeskin cowboy boots (which really looked funny with a robe, but Levis were yet to be invented) handed down from his great[10]-grandfather Adam Bob. Noah Bob was the only man who wasn't given to carousing, drinking to excess, making obscene hand gestures during rush hour traffic, and claiming household pets on his 1040 form. Of course, being around five hundred years old at the time, he needed his sleep and asparagus gave him some kind of terrible gas. Nonetheless, this was the man chosen to assume the awesome task of saving a small remnant of every living creature to repopulate the earth, while heaving violently over the side of a storm-tossed ark.

God was excited about finding this one righteous man and began telling him all about what was to take place. This was a bit disconcerting to Noah Bob since, after Adam Bob, God had decided that He would no longer appear to humans and Noah Bob only heard this loud voice which sounded a lot like James Earl Jones talking about rain, animals, and a boat. Not knowing where the voice was coming from, Noah Bob had those snakeskin boots moving down the road at a pretty good clip. But no matter where or how fast he ran, the voice continued and he finally realized that it must be God because James Earl Jones had entirely too many names to be alive yet.

Noah Bob sat down on a log while God unfolded His plan to him. God was really peeved about man's behavior of late and thought this might be a good time for a scolding, such as wiping everybody and everything off the face of the earth. Besides, He hadn't had a chance to try out this new rain thing, and once it started, it could take as long as forty days or so to turn it off. He was fairly confident that a couple hundred feet of water would go a long way toward cleaning up this mess.

Once again, Noah Bob had reason for concern. Being a farmer with little time for leisure pursuits, he had never gotten around to mastering the art of swimming. He had fallen into the well once but that just amounted to holding on to the sides for a couple of days until somebody dropped the bucket on his head. The thought of dog paddling for several weeks, especially in those boots, had Noah Bob scrambling for alternative punishments involving a lot less water.

Finally, God assured Noah Bob that he was a part of the solution, not the problem, and had virtually nothing to worry about. Part two of the plan involved a very large ocean-going vessel measuring three hundred cubits long by fifty cubits

wide by thirty cubits high. Of course God had to go through the whole routine of what a cubit was, convert it to metric, then to feet, then to more meaningful measurements like "really, really big." The largest boat that Noah Bob had ever seen was probably about the size of a Toyota Corolla, but Noah Bob didn't know that. Why? Because Toyota Corolla had not been invented yet? No! Because Americans were Americans and wouldn't be caught dead driving one of them thar foreign cars. Let's hear it for American Pride! The Heartbeat of America, Ford Tough, Built like a Rock, Studebaker is . . . sorta . . . like a . . . car. Anyway, he hadn't ever seen a very big boat.

When Noah Bob had finally grasped what size boat God had in mind, he immediately felt a whole lot better. It was indeed going to be a fantastic boat, but the fine print was the part about Noah Bob having to build this thing himself . . . in his own backyard . . . during daylight hours . . . with the neighbors watching. It wasn't enough that they constantly snickered about the robe and boots, now he was going to have the U.S.S. *Enterprise* dry docked on his patio.

Sticks and stones and all that stuff was Noah Bob's motto. He was no slacker and immediately got on the phone to Home Depot and ordered eight jillion board feet of gopher wood and several hundred five-gallon buckets of pitch. Being really excited about such a large order, the sales clerk quickly asked Noah Bob for his home address and two credit references and "*What the heck is gopher wood!?*" (Actually what God said was that he would have to "go for" wood, since he obviously didn't have that much on hand.)

When Noah Bob had finally convinced the clerk that he was se-rious, the order was delivered and dumped in the front yard . . . backyard . . . on top of the house. To make matters even worse, his wife, Coraleen, was inside the house watching her afternoon soap operas. Her muffled screams, mixed with the *Days of Our Lives* theme song, could be heard coming from somewhere under the pile of wood. He finally rescued her and, after cleaning off all the pitch, looked at her lovingly and realized just how much better she looked covered in tar. And then, like most wives, she started with the questions. "What are you going to do with all that wood? What do you know about building a boat? Why didn't you get all the tar out of my hair? If I died would you remarry? That probably wasn't even God telling you to do this—you know what a prankster James Earl Jones is. How could you remarry? Do you think you might

be able to get the trash out during our lifetime?" Noah Bob tried to appease her with the old "Honey, I was thinking about maybe a cruise for our three hundredth anniversary." By this time, she was already back in front of the TV watching *As the World Turns.*

CHAPTER III

You Sure These Animals Are Ark-Broken?

ooking at this pile of wood, Noah Bob realized this was quite a task for one man, especially a five hundred-year-old man. He needed some help. Forget the neighbors; they were too busy laughing to be any help. The only help he could count on must come from his own family. After dragging the missus away from the *Soap Opera Awards* long enough to begot three sons, Clarence, Leon, and Willis, Noah Bob took a little break—fifteen to twenty years. Once the boys grew up, he and his hastily conceived offspring began in earnest (given name for his backyard) to build the ark.

They nailed Board A to Joist B. They inserted Pole C into Slot D and fastened securely with a three quarter-inch hex head molly (named for Willis's girlfriend) bolt. Nail. Saw. Hammer. Fasten. Lift that bale. Tote that barge. In only a few months, they had not only learned the first half of the alphabet, but also assembled a gigantic . . . **swingset!?** Whoops! Wrong set of plans. OK Here they are: **Ark**—*some assembly required (approximately 100 years, plus or minus a decade)* Tools required:

Hammer

Saw (or some real fast beavers)

Chisel

Bigger hammer (for those times when "if it don't fit get a . . .")

Shovel

Crane (large white bird to stand on one leg)

Elmer's glue

Pitch (tar) fork

WD-27 (it would be a couple more years before WD-40)

Boom-box (gotta have tunes)

Lots of Band-Aids

Duct tape

Weed whacker

Really, really big hammer

Tweezers

One of those kinda long things that takes two hands to like, you know, turn or hold or something, but you gotta have it.

Work on the ark went slowly at first but gradually began to speed up at second and was flying as we rounded third headed toward the plate for an inside the park home run. "Hey, Three Stooges! Get off that playground and get back over here working on the ark." Of course, having three young men working on the ark, one must be aware that the old "boys will be boys" syndrome can kick in at any time. One morning Noah Bob went out and found that the ark was now equipped with a CD player and several hundred speakers including a nuclear sub-woofer which could bring a camel to his knees in the next county. Leon was running all over the ark trying to find the rear window so that he could install a gun rack. Noah Bob was able to convince him that the gun rack was a bit premature, since firearms would not be along for several hundred more years and then would be mostly decorative in nature until the Chinese finished inventing laundry and take-out and could concentrate on gun powder. And even though he loved Richard Petty as much as Clarence, the giant number 43 painted on the side had to go.

The big boat was really beginning to take shape. As Noah Bob gazed into the shadow it cast over several city blocks, he could make out the dark forms of his neighbors still bent over in convulsive laugh-ter, while their children played merrily on the giant swing set.

With the end in sight, Noah Bob started thinking about relaxing around the pool, shuffleboard with the boys, hors d'oeuvres on the Promenade Deck, and skeet shooting off the fantail. (Skeet were these little round, clay-colored, large, flying hockey-puck-type animals that just really pestered fantails. That's why it was fun, not to mention legal, to blow them to Smithereens, a small village just off the fantail that was known worldwide for its collection of skeet pieces). There was, however, one other little part to the plan that involved some additional passengers, which might somewhat cut into Noah Bob's leisure time.

Part three of the plan, co-authored by a local animal rights group, laid out in minute detail the exact passenger manifest of the ark.

It contained the entire list of names thought up by Adam Bob over half a chapter ago which took several hundred years to complete and would fill numerous volumes with little tiny writing, but we shortened it to avoid a really long and boring chapter. You're welcome.

God didn't want to bother Noah Bob with too many details all at once, so He revealed stages of the plan as needed. He thought the part about all these animal passengers might be better unveiled gradually and while trying to maintain a casual demeanor.

God: "You like animals, right?"

Noah Bob: "Sure. Except for snakes. You know, it's an ancestral thing."

God: "Yeah. No problem. Just thinking, we probably ought to carry a few along on the ark in case later on people want to have zoos, circuses, pets, hamburgers, etc."

Noah Bob: "How many are we talking about here?"

God: "Aw, not that many (God-math for "the San Diego Zoo pales in comparison"). Just a couple of every species on earth."

Noah Bob: "Couldn't hear that last part, but a couple doesn't sound too bad. Might be fun having a diversion. Anything would be better than sitting around listening to Coraleen's griping about the smell of gopher wood."

God: "I'll send them over next Thursday and you can start making friends."

The next Thursday morning, as Noah Bob gazed out of his bedroom window, he saw a line of animals similar to what one might expect at the Rich's One Day sale, except that the animals were much more orderly. They were milling about, plundering the neighbors' garbage cans, and generally fertilizing everything in sight. A pair of hippopotami were lounging in the hot tub next door. The monkeys had somehow managed to crank a Snapper riding mower and were on their way to a new world mulching record. Two elephants were playing catch with a Volkswagen. The homeowners were screaming some rather unflattering epithets at Noah Bob (way beyond the robe and boots stuff) out of second floor windows, which was prudent since there was a Lions Club meeting (with real lions) on the front porch and a rhinoceros falling in love with a gas grill on the back deck.

God tried to reassure Noah Bob. "They usually aren't like this. I think they are just a little excited about going for a boat ride. They're all ark-broken. You just feed them once or twice a day, throw the ball around a little for exercise, and brush their coats (and ties). Really, they won't be any trouble."

"Yea, right!" thought Noah Bob. "First thing we gotta do is get this petting zoo rounded up and into the ark." He and the boys started trying to organize the animals alphabetically. This proved somewhat difficult since not only did most (like some did?) of the animals not know the alphabet, but they also had basically no idea what their names were. This being the case, the men quickly resorted to the "Point and Yell 'Hey You'" system.

"Alligator! Check. Stateroom 103."

"Dodo! Check. Stateroom 113."

"Giraffe! Check. Stateroom 206. Wait a minute! That's not going to work. 'Stretch,' here, is going to have to go in 429 with the vaulted ceiling."

"Jackass! Boy, that drew a crowd. All politicians and talk-show hosts back in line. Check. Stateroom 248."

"Skunk! *WHOA!* We seem to have somewhat of a personal hygiene issue here. Put this aromatic aberration in a room with a window."

"Yak! Zebra! Okay, here's the story. Your reservations got mixed up and we only have one room left for the four of you. It's a suite with a nice fold-out straw pile in the sitting room. You could move to another ark, but I wouldn't recommend it, okay? Thanks for being so understanding. Here you go, tickets to our Las Vegas-style review in the main theater, our treat."

Finally, all the animals were loaded and settled comfortably in their stalls. Noah Bob walked up the street to assure the neighbors that within a couple of days he would take care of all the mess the animals had created. He promised them that it would be washed clean. (har! har!)

Noah Bob was feeling pretty good about how well everything was going when he remembered something God had mentioned earlier that day, or about two paragraphs ago—"Just feed them once or twice a day." "God? This is Noah Bob. How long will this trip last? I gotta have some food for this group. I don't want the tigers looking at me like I'm a sirloin wearing boots."

"Good thinking, Julia Childs. I was hoping that would occur to you before lift-off," God answered in his best Don Rickles voice. "As I told you before, the rain will probably last around forty days or so, which would amount to about 287 billion, trillion gallons of water. Even if nothing gets clogged up, it'll take some time to drain. I haven't finished all the math, but my best guess would be around seven or eight months. You better hit the feed and seed store."

OK, This is going to take a couple of buggies. Willis and Clarence went down the grains aisle: "twelve tons of oats and four thousand bales of hay. That ought to do it. But, what does a gnu eat? Gnuts?" Noah Bob and Leon headed for the carnivore section: "fifteen thousand cans of Alpo, six tons of Kibbles, three tons of Bits, a bag of Milk Bone treats, and a couple of those chew toys. Oh yeah, we gotta have a couple hundred pounds of that kitty litter." No way were they going to sneak through the express line.

Once the groceries were put away, it was time for Noah Bob, his wife, his sons, and their wives to start packing. Aw, man! Willis and Molly (remember the hex head bolt girl?) had never gotten married. You know, career first, waiting for the right time, can't make a commitment, etc. No matter. Before they left, the captain of the ship quickly married them, and Willis played up the part about it being a honeymoon cruise.

Noah Bob and the boys quickly loaded their Samsonite two-suiters and went back to get the ladies' bags. Then they went back and got the elephants to carry the ladies' bags. We're talking trunks, hang-up bags, hat boxes, make-up cases, mountains of shoes, back packs, duffel bags, and of course, seasonal purses containing approximately the same tonnage as a Boeing 747—each. Noah Bob's mind was somewhere between building another ark and imagining life without women when all the ladies graciously agreed to leave two of the hat boxes and didn't really think those purple suede knee boots would come back in style.

Finally, when everyone and everything was on board, God closed the hatch (everyone else had their hands full of luggage). Inside the ark, there was an eerie quietness broken only by the occasional lowing of the cattle, or the cooing of a pigeon, or the raucous laughter of the neighbors having a hurricane party just off the starboard bow. Coraleen, of course, was the first to break the silence: "Noah, go back and get my long flannel night gown, the red one hanging on the back of the bathroom door. You know how cold my feet get in the ocean air! And make sure the oven is off. See if we have any candy or snacks for the trip. Did you *ever* take that trash out? So, where's the rain?" Noah Bob gave his wife an understanding look and thought, "If it weren't for this repopulating thing, you would be fish food!"

CHAPTER IV

Forty-Day Forecast: Wetter Than Normal

hey listened intently for the sound of rain on the roof—or the bottom. You see, it had never rained before and they had no idea exactly where it might come from or how it might sound. Maybe it had already started and sounded like . . . *nothing*. Or maybe that wasn't the neighbors laughing. Maybe it was rain. Naw, Noah

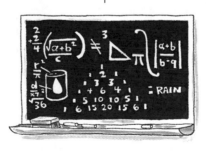

Bob had been listening to the sound of laughter for too long. Wait a minute! Leon heard something like the sound of water falling from a great height. This must be it. But it sounds like its coming from the inside the ark, near the elephants' stall.

"Whoa! Feel better, Dumbo?"

Meanwhile, God was still working out a few of the bugs in the rain formula.

He had used *sine* instead of *cosine* in the condensation theorem, which caused the average raindrop size to be only slightly larger than a Buick. This confusion continues today in trig classes across America, but teachers still will not buy the excuse that not even God understands cosines. It would take a few more days to retool the rainmaking equipment and start the deluge.

Back at the ark, patience was beginning to wear thin. They had played every board game known to man and charades was really difficult since there were no books, movies, or songs at this time. Coraleen had started that stuff about James Earl Jones again and doubted seriously there would ever be anything wet falling from the sky. Willis's wife, Molly, insisted that she was so seasick that death would be a welcome reprieve. She insisted this, in spite of the fact that the ark was not technically "moving."

Suddenly there was a tapping sound on the roof of the ark. Sporadic at first, but gradually increasing into the rhythmic crescendo of a thousand tiny elves tap dancing to a Chuck Berry tune. Could this be rain? Or merely a thousand tiny elves tap dancing to a Chuck Berry tune? Then, through a crack around the door, they could see a brilliant flash of light. Having no previous experience with lightning, they simply assumed that the paparazzi were taking a few more pictures to adorn the front pages of the supermarket tabloids. Even knowing that cameras, and particularly flash bulbs, hadn't been invented yet, they still assumed this. But, mere seconds later, there came a loud cracking noise that sounded like, a really loud . . . uh . . . . . . booming . . . umm . . . . like thunder, okay?

Also, their knowledge of the speed of light versus the speed of sound was somewhat limited, so they did not associate the flash with the boom. They deduced, quite erroneously, that this must be the sound of a really, really, big rain drop. It would take many centuries and many painful experiences before humankind even came close to realizing that although thunder is the loudest, it is lightning that will fry your britches.

We interrupt this program for a special bulletin from the Channel 6 storm watch center: Mostly cloudy with scattered thundershowers, some heavy at times. The storm watch area is eight thousand miles either side of a line from ten miles south-southeast of Kansas City to a point twelve miles east of London to a point twenty-seven miles west of Moscow to Beijing to a point ten miles south-southeast of Kansas City.

Persons in low-lying areas (under 26,000 feet elevation) should be on the lookout for local flooding. We now return you to your regularly scheduled program, already in progress.

After several days of heavy rains, Noah Bob began to experience feelings that were totally unfamiliar to him. These mysterious sensations made his face tighten up, his eyes squint, and his head feel as if it were in a vice. He had discovered one of a number of rather unpleasant side effects of rain—the sinus headache. The others, such as mud puddles, mildew, baseball game delays, ruined car washes, Gene Kelly dances, umbrellas, and sad songs with the word rain in their title, would follow at predetermined intervals throughout history.

In spite of the pain and the ice pack around

his head, he began to detect what he perceived as a slight movement in the floor of the ark. This movement gradually increased until he could tell that the ark was floating freely, rising and falling on the waves, rocking to and fro at the whim of the wind and water. Up. Down. Side to side. This created such a sense of excitement that the entire family, in unison, began that time-honored maritime tradition of enthusiastically blowing lunch in all directions. God reassured them that this minor discomfort would continue only as long as they remained conscious and had an ounce of fluid left in their bodies.

Eventually, everyone's death wish diminished to controlled nausea, and life aboard the ark settled into a daily routine. Noah Bob organized the family into assigned areas of responsibility. Willis was in charge of feeding the animals. Leon shoveled out the stalls and put in fresh straw. Clarence, "Mr. Personality," was assigned the duty of cruise director. The ladies were busy knitting booties and other assorted baby paraphernalia because they knew there would be some furious begotting as soon as this joy ride was over.

Willis really got into his new job and looked very professional in his maître d' outfit. "Hi, I'm Willis. I'll be your waiter this evening. Our specialties include sautéed baby oats served over a bed of new hay with a delightful béarnaise sauce. And for the cats, may I suggest the braised rack of Puss 'n' Boots with peppercorns and brussels sprouts. A light Chianti would be the perfect complement to either meal."

We interrupt this program for a special bulletin from the Channel 6 storm watch center: blubblub, glubblub, blubglubblub, glubglub.

Leon, on the other hand, was less enthralled about his position as a fertilizer executive. Every day, the same thing: shovel out the stall; carry it all the way to the top deck; throw it over the side; see the dead fish. Boy, some of those larger cats really put out a bouquet. Must be the peppercorns and brussels sprouts. He had noticed, however, that he was having a lot less sinus problems than anyone else.

Our cruise director, Clarence, was busy organizing activities and generally trying to keep morale high. He had set up pool-side afternoon mixers so that everyone could make new friends. There was a costume ball on Thursday nights with a door prize for most original outfit. Sports were going pretty well, except basketball. If that rhino does one more lay-up and crashes into the bulkhead, drowning will be the most popular sport.

One morning, as the family crawled out of bed, they noticed a difference in the usual noise level. The elves had stopped tap dancing on the roof. Noah Bob quickly checked his Day Planner and sure enough, forty days right on schedule. Everyone rushed to the top deck and when the hatch had been thrown open, they ran all over the place: jumping, laughing, whoopin and hollerin' like people who had been locked inside for, say . . . , a month and ten days (approximately). Then they ran over to the side and began to vigorously wash their feet. Obviously, Leon had not been swabbing the deck very well after the daily stall cleaning.

Then they looked around at water, water, and more water as far as the eye could see. In every direction there was nothing but water, lots of water. Noah Bob had learned from God about giving out information only on a need-to-know basis. He figured this would be the time to let everyone know that this cruise still had a few more months to go. They all seemed to take the news fairly well, with the possible exception of throwing Noah Bob overboard. (This gave birth to the interoffice memo, whereby the actual person is not directly exposed to angry backlash when delivering bad news.)

At least now they could spend time outside, in the sunshine, on the top deck. They spent their days basking in the warm sun and their nights screaming from the resultant sunburn. This led to the coined phrase that is still popular at beach resorts worldwide, "touch me and die." This routine of basking and screaming helped to pass the time quickly, and after a couple of months not only did their skin look like beef jerky, but there was still water everywhere. This brought about a revival of the popular

"Throw Noah Bob in the Water" game. They searched the vastness of the water for any signs of land or life. One day Leon swore that on the horizon he spotted three other ships. He could make out the names on the sides—*Niña, Pinta,* and *Santa Maria.* But Noah Bob showed him in the *Encyclopedia Britannica* where he was about 6,492 years premature.

Times were growing tense aboard the old ark, and Noah Bob knew he had to do something to restore morale (throwing him in the water helped, but it had to be repeated entirely too often). He decided to send out a dodo bird to see if it could find land. As we all know, and Noah Bob soon discovered, dodos can't fly and this one went over the side and straight to the bottom. Referring back to the two-by-two boarding routine, we know there was only one left, which therefore explains the extinction of the dodo. After some further research, it was determined that doves not only can fly, but also have sense enough to return to the boat if they can't find land. Best of all, somehow more than two doves got aboard allowing room for error. So Noah Bob released a dove. Unfortunately, Willis was shooting skeet off the fantail at the time and, "Pull," BLAM! good-bye dove. Noah Bob had to loose another dove. Word traveled fast aboard the ark, and this dove was reluctant to take flight until he was assured that Willis was securely bound with chains below deck. As the dove soared high into the morning sky and disappeared over the horizon, the hopes of everyone on the ark soared with it. Several hours later, as the exhausted dove crashed back into the deck, (you got it) the hopes of everyone on the ark crashed with it.

This "out-and-back" dove thing went on for a month or so when one day Clarence asked, "Say Daddy, have you noticed that for the last week or so the ark hasn't been moving at all?" Noah Bob pondered that thought. "Do you think it could have something to do with the fact that all the water is gone?" Clarence continued. Prior to rushing to the rail to verify this discovery, Noah Bob took time to reassure Clarence that there were plenty of jobs he could find that did not require advanced skills, such as "actual thinking"—IRS customer service springs to mind.

God called them all over to the rail of the ark because He had a few final words He wanted to say. First of all, He thanked them all for choosing Omnipotent Ark Lines and hoped their cruise had been a pleasant one. Second, don't sweat the dodo extinction thing. It was only a prototype bird contrived by a jokester angel and probably wasn't going to make it much longer anyway. And lastly, they never have to worry about the earth being flooded again. God had come up with some other neat stuff—like fireballs and earthquakes—that was a lot quicker and didn't leave all that mud. As a sign of this promise, every time it rained, He would make a cloud in the shape of a horse or something. Years later, Jesse Jackson changed this to a rainbow because the "Horse or Something" Coalition just didn't have much of a ring to it.

Now it was time to unload the animals and start getting life back to normal. They opened the door, dropped the ramp, and turned to move everybody out in an orderly manner. Narrowly escaping death in the ensuing stampede, Noah Bob decided it would be a good idea to plant a vineyard, grow some grapes, stomp out the juice, let it ferment, and enjoy a cocktail before dinner. After so many years of building the ark, being the neighborhood dunce, riding the waves in the zoomobile, being married to Coraleen, etc., Noah Bob tied on a good one and passed out through October.

Meanwhile, Clarence, Leon, Willis, their aforementioned wives, and the animal couples went their separate ways and began the somewhat daunting task of repopulating the entire planet. When Noah Bob came to, he saw that his sons were doing a good job and really didn't think it necessary for him and Coraleen to jump into the propagation game. He spent the remaining 350 years of his life enjoying solitude and taking out the durn trash. After Noah Bob passed on, Coraleen thought about remarrying, but the dating scene was really depressing, especially when anyone outside her immediate family was at least six hundred years younger. So she died too.

CHAPTER V

How Quickly They Forget

larence, Leon, and Willis, with dedicated support from their wives, did a commendable job of bringing the census figure of "8" just after the flood to a respectable "whole bunch" in just a few hundred years. Obviously there was no late night television to interfere, and God had put a temporary "cease and desist order" on the headache for this period of time in order to speed up repopulation. The only exception being Molly, who still complained of occasional bouts of seasickness.

The animals were also doing their part to reestablish the animal kingdom. The carnivores were especially anxious to repopulate as expeditiously as possible, because they were on a veggie diet until everyone was off the "endangered species" list. A lion munching on sunflower seeds just doesn't project that "King of Beasts" image.

Unfortunately, it didn't take very long for people to once again, begin acting like, well, people. Things were going pretty well and life was so easy that they had plenty of time to sit around inflating their personal egos (a Latin term for "am I good or what?"). They had so much spare time that they decided to build a giant tower that would reach all the way to heaven (or at least above the high water mark of the recent flood). This thing was about halfway up when God decided that He had better stop this before it got so high that all these nitwits fell off and broke their necks. Just for fun He invented a bunch of new languages and had everybody speaking in a different tongue. When one guy asked for a hammer in French, it might sound to the Spanish guy like "Your sister is so ugly, she couldn't get a date with a possum!" Then the "defend your family honor" fisticuffs would commence. Pretty soon, the only con-

struction going on was remodeling each other's dental work, and the tower was a thing of the past. Years later it was moved to Italy and even though it leaned a little to one side became a famous tourist attraction.

Even though God knows everything, it was still hard for Him to believe that man had such a short memory. It had only been a few hundred years since He had gently reminded people to behave, and now they were up to their old tricks again. Since total annihilation had not worked, He was going to have to come up with some new approach to get His creations to "act right."

He decided to take some time to think about this and went down to Jekyll Island, just south of Savannah, to relax and play a little golf. Keeping with His policy of not appearing publicly, He disguised Himself as Sam Snead (who was alive at the time but playing on the European tour) and headed for the links. But when you're God, not even golf is much of a challenge. So after shooting a 73 on 72 holes (He would have had a perfect 72, but on the last hole He just had to try that one iron), He went back to pondering what to do about mankind. He remembered a conversation with a couple of guys in His foursome about a good ol' boy who had just moved from Jekyll Island to Atlanta. They talked about how this fellow never tried to sandbag his handicap; didn't use a foot wedge in the woods when no one was looking; didn't talk out loud when someone else was teeing off; didn't cuss when he sliced one in the water; and as far as they knew, he pretty much ran his business and life the same way. Heck of a fellow, although they hated playing golf with him, because he insisted on playing by the rules and maintaining proper golf etiquette.

This gave God an idea. Maybe if He used a straight-up man like this to lead a group of His hand-picked people, they could set an example for the rest of the world. Since He didn't have anyone else in mind, this fellow just might be a good one with whom to start. "What was his name? Started with an A. They said something about his being the great, great something grandson of Noah Bob's son, Clarence. Oh well, I'll think of it on My way to Atlanta."

God found Abraham Bob right where one would expect. Stuck in traffic, on the I-75/ I-85 connector, right in the middle of downtown. The poor fellow was trying to get a load of hogs to the farmer's market at high noon in the hot July sun. And the people stuck around him weren't too thrilled about the fragrant bouquet radiating from his passengers. Folks were honking their horns (yet another little known fact: horns were invented before cars), yelling some very unflattering stuff about his family history, and using some limited but effective sign language (this was the first recorded occurrence of "Road Rage"). Ignoring the discord around him, Abraham Bob calmly sat listening to Ernest Tubb belt out "Walking the Floor Over You." Again, radios had not been invented. This was the real Ernest Tubb singing to the hogs from the back of the wagon.

God was indeed impressed with Abraham Bob's kind, gentle, and calm nature and decided that

this was definitely His man. As usual, He immediately started telling Abraham Bob all about His plans for him and the Chosen People. Abraham Bob responded with "Ernest, what in the world are you talking about?" After this exchange went on for several minutes, Abraham Bob realized that it wasn't Ernest talking and must be somebody stuck in traffic around him. But they all had their windows rolled up and were too busy gasping for air to complete a sentence. Finally, God identified Himself. When Abraham Bob came to, God assured him that He meant him no harm and as soon as he dropped off those stinking hogs, they needed to have a serious conversation.

When Abraham Bob got back to the house, God was waiting for him in the swing on the front porch. He couldn't see anybody, but since the swing was moving pretty good, he

assumed that must be where God was sitting. God also told him that He would wait while he got a bath. The hog aroma was still hanging tough.

Clean and refreshed with a big glass of iced tea—with lots of lemon and just slightly less sweet than cane syrup, but almost as thick—Abraham Bob sat down to listen to what God had in store for him. Since the swing was still moving, he faced that direction. But the voice seemed to be in "surround sound," and one minute it was coming out of the chimney and the next somewhere in the chicken house—where egg laying was at an all-time high that afternoon. "What started out as a simple idea to have a fishing buddy," God began, "is getting out of hand. I thought the first batch of people might have just been a fluke, so I picked the cream of the crop, Noah Bob, and wiped out everyone and everything else. Now only a short time later, mankind is back to their old tricks of acting like a bunch of drunken sailors."

"What I have in mind," God continued, "is to concentrate on one group of folks. When I get them to doing right and following My directions, then they can be an example to the rest of the world. I want you, Abraham Bob, to be the father of that group who will for all times be known as the Partridge Family. No, wait, that's already reserved for a TV show several thousand years from now. How about the Chosen People? Not too catchy, but conveys the meaning pretty well."

Abraham Bob was not only extremely flattered that God would choose him for this honor, but also thoroughly confused as to what his particular duties would be and why his tea was so sweet. As for being the father of this group, Abraham Bob and his wife, Sara Jean, didn't have any children of their own, and since they were well into their seventies, had pretty much discounted the idea of having a family about thirty years ago. God told him not to worry, that he and Sara Jean would still have a passel of offspring.

After a good chuckle about having children at their age, Abraham Bob agreed to follow God's directions and asked, "What do You want me to do?"

God was pleased with Abraham Bob's obedient response. "First thing, change your name. Your new name will be Abe. It will be a lot shorter, easier to embroider on your work shirts, and appeal to the common man if you ever decide to run for president."

"Awright," agreed Abraham Bob.

"Second," God went on, "move from Atlanta to a new place that I have picked out for you."

CHAPTER VI

The Official Birth
Of The Rednecks

be (see how quickly he caught on to the new name) didn't mind moving because he was sick and tired of hauling hogs through downtown Atlanta. It didn't really much matter to him, but he thought he ought to ask, "Where to?"

"Don't worry about where," God answered. "Just head down I-85 south and I'll tell you when you get there."

Abe loaded up Sara Jean; his nephew, Leroy; all the farm hands that wanted to go; several hundred head of hogs; three milk cows; two mules; and his coon dog, Bullet; and headed South. After traveling for several days, they came to a lovely village situated on top of the plains. There were friendly tigers roaming freely through the streets, eagles circling overhead, and plainsmen hanging out in coffee houses cramming for final exams. He decided to name it after the original color of Sara Jean's hair—Auburn.

God told him that this was the place He wanted Abe to settle down and raise a family. Also to his future generations He would give all the land from the Chattahoochee River on the east to the Tombigbee River on the west, and from the Gulf of Mexico on the south, to the Great Smoky Mountains on the north. Abe was pleased with the land that God had promised, but he and Sara Jean, both now pushing eighty years old, again had a good laugh about the future generation thing. God, having extremely good hearing, told them He really didn't appreciate the laughing, and at the right time they would have a young'un.

About this time, Leroy began to miss some of the conveniences he had enjoyed in the big city and decided to move off to the twin cities

of Sodom and Gomorrah. This area was brimming with shopping and entertainment, and Leroy and his family started living the high life. The problem was that these two cities were also way yonder overstocked with beer joints, pool halls, gambling casinos, discount outlets, lawyers, and other perversions about which God was not real thrilled. God had been watching this corruption going on for about as long as He could tolerate it and had decided it was time to clean up this mess. Since Leroy was Abe's favorite nephew, He did get word to him that it might be a good idea to pack up, move out, and don't look back.

God had promised not to flood things again, so He had to come up with a different way to resolve this little problem. Turns out that there was a fireworks stand about every thirty yards around both cities. One little "accidental" spark in one of them set off a chain reaction that lit up the sky way past Chattanooga. Leroy's wife, Epsom, just couldn't help herself and had to turn around, just in time to see Sears and Roebuck and Rahab's House of Nails go up in flames. Since God had included a "no peek" clause in the agreement, Epsom was immediately turned into a box of salt. Leroy kept his eyes straight ahead and didn't even know his wife was missing for three days.

Several centuries later, after the ashes had cooled sufficiently, both cities were rebuilt on the same site but with new names—Columbus and Phenix City. Must have been something in the soil because in the early twentieth century both returned to pretty much the same level of corruption that caused their original demise.

Back in the Loveliest Village of the Plains, one morning Sara Jean awoke bright and early, looked outside at the dawn of a beautiful new day, and threw up! She felt much better after a hearty breakfast of cereal, toast, pickled herring, chocolate pudding, and a caramel spinach soufflé. Her day went well, except for the occasional outbursts of uncontrollable crying, laughing, and throwing of fine china and muffin tins at Abe.

Several days of this threatening behavior led Abe to suggest that they should talk—he suggested this from just out of range of flying kitchenware. What could be causing these erratic mood swings? And with her recent dietary cravings, she had been putting on weight like the *Titanic* taking on water.

Whoa! Morning sickness? Mood swings? Weight gain? What we have here is a 100 year-old expectant mother. Somebody get on the phone to the *National Enquirer*. We got a winner here. God, of course, just smiled His "I told you so" smile.

The next nine months were busy indeed for the mother-to-be. She had to pick an obstetrician; buy new maternity robes; decorate the nursery; intermittently throw up; continually try to convince people that she is really a *pregnant old lady* and not a *fat old lady*; take Lamaze classes; cry at unspecified times and in response to nothing in particular; hire a diaper service; congratulate and berate Abe daily for doing this to a woman her age.

Finally, the glorious day arrived—the Rich's One Day sale. Unfortunately, Sara Jean went into labor and had to miss it. When they arrived at the hospital, Sara Jean was immediately wheeled into the gastro-intestinal wing and they began trying to relieve what was thought to be an extreme build-up of gases from too much Mexican food. "If you don't get me to the maternity ward before this baby, or my lawyer, arrives, I will own this place, and if this pain doesn't let up soon, I am going to personally rip your eyes out!" Sara Jean said politely.

After several hours of rather intense labor, Sara Jean requested a mild sedative that would hopefully render her unconscious until sometime after the child started fifth grade. Soon the son that God had promised arrived. A healthy baby boy who looked exactly like his father—bald and extremely wrinkled. As Abe held his son for the first time, he gave him the name that he had always wanted to be called— Bubba. He also thought it would be a good time to get this name on the birth certificate before Sara Jean regained consciousness. She had insisted that Ulysses S. would be a good successor to Abe (a little Civil War humor).

God's idea for selecting a special group of people to be His own was proceeding according to plan. Abe had followed His commands, changed his name, moved to a new place, and now a son had been born to carry on the plan. God was so pleased that he decided it was time to give His people a symbol that would set them apart from all others and continually remind them that they were His. Abe thought this was a good idea and asked what kind of mark God had in mind. "Well, actually I had been thinking that circumcision might be an appropriate badge," God answered.

"Sounds good to me," said Abe. "Just exactly what is circumcision?"

After God finished explaining and as soon as Abe could straighten up and catch his breath again, he asked "Could I, uh, get back to You on that?" Abe knew he had to do some fast thinking. Surely there must be some other sign that would do just as well without fooling around with that part of a man's body. He went out into the field where it was quiet and he could concentrate. He sat with his head bowed in his hands and tried to come up with some suitable alternative. Tattoo? Naw, they'd get confused with sailors and circus sideshow folks. Feathers in their hair? Nope, the Indians already had that one. Red dot between their eyes? Other Indians had that one. The hot sun beat down on his back, but he continued to ponder. There had to be another way. Shave their heads? Hare Krishnas. Boy, that sun was hot! Wear a baseball cap at all times? They already did that. He just couldn't come up with anything that he thought God might accept. And besides, he was really getting blistered.

The next morning he met with God to tell Him that he had failed to find a suitable alternative and they might as well get on with the cutting. Before he could say a word, God commented on how sunburned his neck was and how it looked almost like some kind of red insignia. A red insignia? Like a sign? It was worth a try. "That's the sign I came up with," Abe said, tentatively.

To Abe's surprise, God liked the idea. "From now on, that will be not only the sign, but also the name of My Chosen People," God declared. The Rednecks were now an official nation—labeled by accident, but Southern by the Grace of God.

CHAPTER VII

Desperate Times Call
For Desperate Measures

ow that the Redslecks had achieved the status of most favored nation with the One by whom you would most like to be most favored, and they had been given a sizable tract of land upon which to build their nation, not to mention old Abe and Sara Jean somehow at their age having Bubba to carry on the Redneck name it would be almost impossible not to notice what a really, really, long run-on sentence we have here.

Time, as well as sentences, was running on and before you knew it, Abe's son, Bubba, was of marrying age. One of Abe's farm hands told Bubba about this fine looking little girl he had run across while picking up a load of sweet feed for the mules down in Loachapoka. Besides looks, she had a lot of other good qualities too, like her daddy owned the feed store—meaning he was pretty well off. Best of all, he thought maybe she was a not-too-distant cousin, so he would be marrying within the family.

Bubba thanked him, grabbed the fastest mule in the barn, and tore out for Loachapoka. This particular mule could fly like the wind and was just about as hard to stop. He came through the front door of the feed store at seventy miles an hour and did about twelve hundred dollars worth of damage before Bubba could slow him down up against the back wall. Fortunately, Reba (the aforementioned "fine looking little girl") was much impressed with Bubba's riding skill and accepted his proposal right on the spot.

After helping her daddy clean up the store and catching that mule, Bubba and Reba had twin sons— Jake and Ernest (named after his daddy's favorite country singer). Ernest happened to be the oldest by a minute or two and as was the cus-

tom, stood to inherit the family business when Bubba passed on. Ernest was also his daddy's favorite, because he could plow a pair of new mules with one hand and field dress a deer with the other while singing Ernest Tubb's "Walking the Floor Over You" out of one side of his mouth and spitting Red Man out of the other.

Jake, on the other hand, was more of a mama's boy. He hung around the house, played on the piano, and helped his mama make quiche and fancy pastries. Reba was determined that just because Jake was a little on the sissy side, he wasn't going to lose out on all of his daddy's inheritance. So one day, while they were whipping up a succulent chocolate soufflé, she devised a plan to fool Bubba into giving everything to her favorite son. Jake went out to the barn and rubbed around on some sweaty mules (he couldn't catch that fast one) to simulate Ernest's aroma. He then put a little pinch of Skoal between cheek and gum and began to whistle show tunes. "Country music, you idiot, country music!" corrected Reba.

Then, much to their mutual disgust, they fixed a big pot of possum and taters for Bubba. When Jake carried it in, his daddy's head went straight in the trough. That possum and taters, along with the smell of mule sweat and the sound of country music, was so good that Bubba thought he had already passed away and gone to heaven. So when Jake, in his best Ernest imitation, asked about the inheritance, Bubba unhesitatingly, although mistakenly, signed everything over to him.

Their scheme had worked to perfection with only one potentially minor problem—Ernest would be home soon, and when he learned about this little deception, he probably was going to be just a tad upset. He might lose control and accidentally put a serious butt whuppin' on his baby brother. Jake, being somewhat fragile and opposed to receiving much physical abuse, quickly threw a few things in a duffel bag, caught the next fastest mule, and headed out to seek his fortune while Ernest cooled off.

Assuming that it would be the last place that Ernest would look for him, Jake headed north. His mama had an uncle around Louisville, and maybe he could stay there awhile until it was safe to return home. Even on a fast mule Louisville was about a two week trip, but Jake enjoyed the beautiful scenery of the mountains and took time to fulfill the never-ending appeal painted on every barn and birdhouse in the southeastern United States: "See Rock City."

About halfway to his uncle's, Jake stopped at a roadside Camp 'n Cook for the night. After sampling some homemade elixir from a mason jar offered by the campground proprietor, he fell into a deep sleep and began to dream of strange and mysterious things. He saw people dressed in sparkling costumes and large hats. They were climbing steps up to a big stage in front of a lot of other folks. There the performers, accompanied by stringed instruments, made strange twanging noises about pickup trucks, old dogs, and love gone bad. It was a grand ole sight. The next morning, when Jake's head cleared enough to identify solid objects, he made a pile of stones in the shape of a guitar and named the place Ralphburgen. Years later, the residents finally figured out that this was only a noise Jake was making with his head hanging in a bucket and renamed the city Nashville.

After several more days of travel, Jake arrived at his uncle's house outside Louisville. He explained to his Uncle Louis (why did you think they called it Louisville?) about the situation back home and asked if he could hang out there awhile; he would be willing to work for his keep. Uncle Louis had a good-sized farm and assured Jake that he had plenty of work for him, and he could stay as long as he needed.

During the next month or so, Uncle Louis noticed that Jake was a pretty good worker and offered to pay him for his labor. Jake had a deal for him. By this time, he had gone and fallen head over heels in love with his cousin, Ray Nell, Uncle Louis's youngest daughter. "I'll keep working for you for nothing but room and board if you'll let me marry your daughter, my cousin," Jake told him.

Uncle Louis was fond of his nephew, but wasn't sure he wanted him for a son-in-law. Besides, what would that make them, uncle 'n' father-in-law and nephew 'n' son-in-law? "Tell you what I'll do," countered Uncle Louis. "You work for me for seven years, we'll get to know each other a little better, and then you can marry my daughter" (see, cousin marrying *is* scriptural!). Seven years was a long time, but Jake was *some kind of* in love with Ray Nell so he agreed.

He worked hard tending the livestock, plowing the fields, and occasionally catching a few minutes with Ray Nell behind the barn. Before he knew it, seven years had passed, and it was time for the big day. Kin folks gathered from miles in every direction. A sumptuous reception feast was prepared, which included cheese straws, a fruit bowl, some of them little weenies, pickled pigs feet, two huge bowls of butter beans, and a pecan pie.

As the preacher droned on about "leaving and cleaving" and "for this and for that," Jake's mind had already wandered off to the honeymoon, and he barely got the "I do's" in the right place. Finally, he heard the part about "you may kiss your bride." Jake puckered up, closed his eyes, whipped that veil off her face, and put a double lip lock on his new bride. Something wasn't right! Ray Nell's normal honey dew lips tasted more like mule feed. And he sure didn't remember her having that much of a mustache.

Opening one eye slowly, he recognized his spouse of thirty seconds as Ray Nell's older sister, Lee Ann. Except for the excess amount of facial hair and breath bad enough to melt pig iron, Lee Ann wasn't a bad looking woman. This wasn't, however, the deal Jake thought he had made. When he confronted Uncle Louis, his uncle referred him back two paragraphs to the part where he said, "marry your daughter." Jake made a mental note to be *way more* specific next time about which daughter.

He had forgotten that it was customary for the older sister to get married first, and with Lee Ann's beard and breath, her chances for matrimony (without some serious deception) were slim; however, his uncle agreed to let Jake marry his Ray Nell next week if he would work for him another seven years.

(Back in those days it was even alright to have more than one cousin as a wife at the same time.) Jake agreed and the next Saturday he finally got to marry Ray Nell. You better believe this time he looked under the veil *before the wedding.*

Lee Ann was just a little jealous because she knew that Jake loved Ray Nell the most. So to try to win her husband's favor, she set about seeing just how many sons she could turn out in the shortest amount of time. Jake was pretty much wore out, but you couldn't get that grin off his face with a cutting torch. Lee Ann was leading by ten to nothing before Ray Nell finally figured out that sleeping with her husband was not enough; they had to actually have sex. Strangely enough, this helped tremendously and Ray Nell finally gave birth to a couple of boys. Before this little rivalry finally played out, there were an even dozen towheads tearing around their doublewide and eating them out of house and home.

Raising twelve boys is not an easy task, even with two mothers. Jake tried to treat his sons as equally as possible, but he just couldn't help being somewhat partial to Joe Bob, Ray Nell's first boy—mainly because Jake liked Joe Bob's mama the best, and secondly, because he was a lot like his daddy when he was a boy. While the other roughnecks were working in the fields or generally terrorizing the whole trailer park, he preferred to hang around the house, think deep thoughts, watch *Jeopardy*, and expound on how he was going to be "somebody" when he grew up.

To make matters worse, Joe Bob was elected Homecoming King, and Jake bought him a brand new powder blue double-knit leisure suit with navy stitching to wear to the big dance. It made the other boys, in their ragged, wore-out overalls, madder than a bunch of wet settin' hens. They vowed then and there that when the chance arose, they were going to do in "Mr. Smarty Britches."

One day the boys were working way over in the back pasture dipping some cows in creosote. When they looked up, they saw a vision of powder blue coming down the road. About that same time, they heard the train whistle of the northbound *Louisville Flyer*, which stopped to take on water less than a quarter mile across the field from where they were working. They also remembered from the morning newspaper that the Ringling Brother (there was only one of them at this time) Circus was on the train headed up north to start the summer tour. This fact was further confirmed by the fragrant aroma emanating from a number of well-

fed pachyderms. Now for a bunch of Rednecks with somewhat limited mental capacity, those fellas quickly put together an elaborate plan to rid themselves of their brat brother. First, they stripped off that leisure suit and dipped Joe Bob in the creosote vat. Then they shaved two coon dogs and stuck the hair all over him. One of them grabbed a banana from his lunch sack, stuck it

in Joe Bob's mouth, and they took off toward the tracks. The first circus fellow they ran up on, fortunately, wasn't exactly a mental giant either and fell for the story about Joe Bob's being a talking gorilla. He gave them thirty-five dollars and threw his new pet in a boxcar just as the *Flyer* pulled out.

The boys were feeling right proud of themselves until somebody mentioned that their daddy just might notice when his favorite son didn't show up around the house for a week or two, and they had better come up with some kind of explanation. Looking toward their futures as politicians and used car salesmen, they immediately decided to go with the old reliable "half-truth." Handing the powder blue ensemble to their daddy, they allowed as to how they were sitting there having lunch out of their syrup buckets when Joe Bob suddenly took this freak notion to join the circus. They tried to stop him, but he tore out of his clothes, jumped butt-naked on the moving train, and by now was halfway across Ohio headed for parts unknown. It was just pure luck that they weren't killed by the train and even better luck that they found that thirty-five dollars between the tracks.

Jake was emotionally tore-up. He had always had high hopes of Joe Bob's turning out to be a doctor or a professor or a game show host, and now he had run off with the circus. As if that weren't bad enough, Jake had to try to figure out why his coon dogs were going bald.

CHAPTER VIII

Amongst The Yankees

s the train lurched its way northward, Joe Bob had a lot of time to think about his future and to wonder exactly what life would be like as a talking gorilla. What does a gorilla talk about? Could he get anything to eat besides bananas? When would this hair stop itching? In spite of the dire circumstances, there were some lighter moments in the old boxcar. He was in with a bunch of fun-loving elephants who seemed to get a charge out of squirting him with trunk loads of water. Not being very observant, Joe Bob never noticed just how much of the creosote and hair was washing away. When the train pulled into the station, the man who had bought him opened up the large door. He asked Joe Bob if he had seen a talking gorilla and did he know that he was naked. Nudity has a definite effect on speed and Joe Bob tore out of there like his britches (if he had had any on) were on fire.

Some time later, after acquiring a new wardrobe off an unwatched clothesline, Joe Bob came to the realization that it would be necessary not only to get out his resume and start interviewing but also to ask around in regards to just exactly where the heck he was. The people here seemed to speak a different language, and he had a hard time understanding what they were saying. But they seemed to like the way he talked and kept asking him to repeat certain words like "y'all" and "over yonder," after which they would laugh and laugh. It took some doing, but finally he was able to figure out that he had landed in New Jersey (see *Hinterlands*, Chapter I), and these people were known as *Yankees*.

He soon realized that if he was going to fit in there, the "Bob" had to go and he would be known only as "Joe." He would have to talk a lot faster and learn the northerly art of impatience, as well as a certain degree of rudeness. Another essential skill to be mastered was swift and obnoxious horn blowing. Cars were yet to be invented, but Yankees were already in love with honking.

Joe (Joey to his closest friends) promptly adopted these required character flaws and landed a job at the brick factory. Being a quick study, his knowledge of brick making and office politics increased rapidly. In no time at all he was sprinting up the corporate ladder and beginning to be noticed by top management—in this case, all members of the Roe Family. Their grandfather, He Roe, had founded the business seventy years ago and now Roe Industries produced 90 percent of the bricks in the known world.

As sometimes happens (more often in politics and televangelism

than in business), a man's meteoric rise can be brought to an abrupt halt by a woman. Seems that Corn Roe, the wife of the big boss, Zo, took a liking to Joey and thought they should get a little better acquainted outside office hours at her secret downtown apartment. Now Joe, being an upright young man with quality raising, knew right from wrong and turned her down flat. He insisted that the rejection was motivated purely by morals and had nothing to do with the fact that she was uglier than a slaughter house. But, a woman scorned . . . She lied and told her husband that Joe had made a pass at her and should be fired. Zo wasn't blind and knew that Joe wasn't either, but he had to do something to appease this screaming woman. He put Joe back on the third shift cleaning dandruff and small vermin out of the other workers' hard hats.

But, lest we forget, Joe was one of God's Chosen People, and He wasn't about to leave him buried on the third shift. Word begin to circulate around the plant that there were some serious problems in the department in charge of smelting pig iron. Well, Joe had had plenty of experience *smelling* pigs back on his daddy's farm and figured *smelting* had to be similar. With a mostly lucky guess about adding just a pinch of oregano and baking at 425 degrees for one hour, he solved the problem. The big boss was so impressed that he put Joe in charge of all the business, divorced that ugly wife, and took off on a cruise with his young secretary.

Meanwhile, the economy of the South was experiencing a downturn, or as technically defined by financial analysts, "going down the toilet." They would have called it the Great Depression, but it wasn't time for that yet. So they just called it the Great Going Down the Toilet. Times were so bad that in order to survive many Southerners were having to perform that most despicable act of—you got it—going up north. With hat in hand they were trekking up to Yankeeland to look for work. It don't get no worse than that!

Jake and his family were really feeling the pinch, and much to his dismay, he had to send his ten oldest boys up north to look for work. Having no money for a train ticket and wanting to save their frequent flyer miles for a trip to Vegas, the boys had to come up with an inexpensive way to get up north. Remembering the trick they had used with Joe Bob, they stripped off their clothes and covered themselves with creosote. Since the coon dogs had never been able to grow back all their hair again, the desperate boys had to shave a cou-

ple of goats to cover themselves with hair. Fortunately, the same circus guy was at the train stop and once again fell for the old *talking gorilla* routine.

This was an especially tough time on old Jake. He still wasn't totally over the loss of Joe Bob and now ten more of his sons had been taken from him leaving only the youngest, Ben, at home. Jake spent the next several weeks tearing his clothes and grieving about not only his loss, but now whatever had caused his coon dogs to go bald had gotten into his goats.

Meanwhile, back on the train the boys had noticed that the circus guy, afraid of losing his talking gorillas again, was keeping a pretty close eye on them. So, as the train was slowing down for the last stop, they figured that it might be a good idea to sneak out the top of the boxcar and run for the woods.

Finding a job up north was not nearly as easy as they had thought it would be. They left applications at every business they came by and went on numerous interviews—with no luck. After several weeks, the youngest brother suggested that they might have a better chance of getting human-type work if they cleaned off the creosote and goat hair—out of the mouths of babes. The very next job for which they applied was at the brick factory, and they were all invited back for a second interview.

Sure enough, when they showed up the next day, who should be sitting behind the desk—PUBLIC SERVICE ANNOUNCEMENT: For those of you who haven't figured out what happens next, *Wheel of Fortune* is probably way over your head—but their long lost brother. Trying to fit in with his Yankee environment, Joe Bob had changed quite a bit over the years. The boys didn't recognize him with his thin little mustache, horn-rimmed glasses, and pocket protector, but something about that new three-piece powder blue double-knit business suit sure did look familiar. Joe Bob could tell they had no idea who he was and decided to have a little fun with them. He told them that the only job openings available were for a company football team. But there were only ten of them. They needed one more player. Did they have any other brothers down home who might join them? The boys reluctantly told him that there was one more brother, but they didn't think their daddy would let him go this far from home. Joe Bob asked if there had been any other brothers. They said there was one other, but several years ago he suddenly turned into a gorilla and they hadn't seen him since.

The only way Joe Bob would give them work was if they could get that other brother up there to fill out the rest of the team. They knew they must return home and bring Ben back with them, but there just wasn't any creosote and goat hair to be found in New Jersey. Finally they got their daddy to accept a collect call and advised him of the situation. Jake didn't want Ben playing no football, particularly in no New Jersey, but times were getting tougher every day. There didn't seem to be any other choice, so he would be coming up with Ben and maybe get hired on as coach or something.

When Jake and Ben arrived in New Jersey, the other boys met them at the station and they all went directly to the brick factory. Joe Bob was so glad to see his daddy and baby brother again, that he whipped off his glasses, threw the pocket protector out the window, shaved his mustache, and told them who he was. There was a whole lot of hugging and crying and catching up on everything that had happened since his brothers had shipped him off with the circus. Joe Bob assured his older brothers that he had forgiven them and gave them jobs on the spot—third shift, cleaning out them hard hats.

CHAPTER IX

This Figa Roe Ain't About Singing

he Great Going Down the Toilet continued to plague the South. Corn dried up in the field, boll weevils ate the cotton, fish wouldn't bite, and nobody could even spell job, never mind find one. Word got back home about how well Jake, Joe Bob, and the rest of the boys were doing up north. With things so bad, little by little more folks decided to try their luck above the Mason-Dixon line. This trickle soon became a flood as ever increasing numbers left the Land of Grits and Gravy for the Land of Jobs and Traffic.

The Rednecks adapted fairly well to their new environment, with the exceptions of the cold weather and people calling them "youse guys." They performed well at their jobs at the brick factory, and some moved on up the ladder into management positions. New generations were born that had never seen the South, but they learned about their proud heritage at their parents' knees. They were taught to observe the sacred holidays—the opening day of deer season and the Daytona 500. You can take the Redneck out of the South, but you can't take the South out of the Redneck.

When Zo Roe returned with his new wife to run the family business, his newfound state of marital bliss overflowed into how well he treated his employees. Unfortunately, as time passed, Mr. Zo—as people are prone to do—did too. The position of Chairman of the Board of Roe Industries was passed to his son, Ze.

Unlike his kindly father, Ze Roe was a man driven not only by a full-time chauffeur but also by greed and distrust. He was afraid there might be several dollars somewhere in the world that didn't have his fingerprints on them, and he had a bad case of dislike and distrust for the Rednecks. This was a bad combination, and the Chosen People soon began to feel an ill wind blowing from the executive offices. At first they thought that Ze had just had too much Mexican refried beans for lunch but soon realized

that this wind might be a sign of hard times to come.

The next Thursday, around half past nine in the morning, times got harder than a week-old biscuit. Due to supposed economic conditions, Ze announced that Roe industries would be going through a period of restructuring and downsizing. A number of middle management positions would be abolished and the schedules of a large number of other employees would be rearranged. Strangely enough, the only employees affected by these changes were of the Redneck persuasion. They all wound up on the—you guessed it—third shift. And just to make sure that none of them would break in line in front of his wife at Neiman Marcus, they all got a cost of living decrease of about 50 percent.

Everybody was hoppin' mad and on the verge of telling Roe what he could do with his jobs. Then they remembered how bad things still were down South, and they really didn't have anywhere to go. It was impossible to make ends meet on the low wages. They had barely enough to eat. The children were dressed in rags. Shoes were only a distant memory. Even those who had the courage to leave were so indebted to the company credit union that quitting would have meant going directly to debtors' prison. There was no escape from this intolerable life of poverty and suffering. Fortunately, about this time, I became really depressed and decided to change the subject.

One of the Redneck women, affectionately known as Mama to her thirteen children, was down at the river doing her usual weekly clothes washing. All of the children, except the two youngest, were either in school or at work or should have been at one of those two. As she pounded the clothes with a rock and rinsed them clean in the river water, she wondered quietly why she had not just gone down the street to the Laundromat. Sure it was crowded, noisy, and the change machine never worked, but at least there was no pounding with a rock.

As she continued this stupid routine, the next-to-youngest child, affectionately known as No. 12, asked her mother rather matter-of-factly if she could have some gum and if she knew that the baby carriage was floating about halfway across the river. Another good reason to go to the Laundromat—your children don't float off.

They both watched helplessly as the carriage headed toward the opposite shore. It was almost run over by a speeding garbage scow and then floated directly into the path of a school of mullet on a field trip.

Miraculously, it eventually glided up onto the beach in front of a group of surprised onlookers. The baby was unhurt but screaming like a banshee from being splashed by the inconsiderate mullet.

Coincidentally, in this group of curious bystanders was Cai Roe, the oldest daughter of Mr. Ze. Cai was a single girl, nearing old maid status, due in part to the fact that most suitors were intimidated by the power and position of her father. The other part was that Cai held a remarkable resemblance to Uga (mascot for the Georgia Bulldogs). She frequently came to the river to flirt with the merchant marines on vessels anchored away from the shore. From that distance and with the help of a little fog, her appearance was greatly enhanced and occasionally some of the more desperate sailors might even wave back.

As they pulled the carriage out of the water, Cai was struck by the courage and boldness exhibited by this tiny child. He seemed brave, not so much because of his reaction to the frightening experience of crossing the river, but because he could look straight into her bulldog face without so much as a whimper. Cai had a thought. It was beginning to look doubtful that she was ever going to be able to attract a husband. Maybe this was at least God's way of giving her a child. She cradled him in her arms and started to think of a name for her baby. "Let's see, he came from the water and was screaming at the top of his lungs," she thought. "I'll call him Figa (Yankee for 'sings like a carp'), Figa Roe. Kinda has an operatic ring to it."

Mama and No. 12 watched as they carried the baby off to the big house. She would miss him, but with twelve already at home, she had more than she could handle. Besides, he would grow up in a life of privilege and have all the finer things that she couldn't afford to give him. And if her quickly hatched plan worked, she would be able to spend plenty of time with him anyway.

The next morning, bright and early, Mama showed up at the big house and applied for the job of nanny. After the butler led her out to the back pasture and put a bell around her neck, she explained, "Not the *goat-type* nanny, but the *baby sitter-type*." After a thorough interrogation to determine that she wasn't just another talking goat, he ushered her into the house to meet with the new mother. Cai entered the room with baby Figa in her arms. She handed him to Mama and was amazed at how he immediately took to this strange, new woman. Cai hired Mama on the spot.

From then on Mama had her hands full. She got up early, cooked breakfast, and got the other twelve off for the day. Then she went to the big house where she spent the rest of the day taking care of Figa. The first thing she did was pick a new name for her son. She needed a good Redneck name that would denote strength, character, intelligence, cloven hooves, large flat antlers, and be easy to spell. "Maybe something from the animal kingdom would work," she thought. "How about . . . Moose, that's it." She could only use this name in secret, but the baby seemed to really take to it. She also taught him about his Redneck heritage and instilled in him all the Southern values, customs, and traditions.

CHAPTER X

The Moose
Is Aloose

oose grew into a handsome, intelligent, and polished young man and was the pride of the Roe family. Even Mr. Ze was right fond of Figa, primarily because his other grandson looked and talked a lot like Yul Brenner. Figa attended all the finest schools, made straight As, excelled at sports, and was voted "Most Likely to Part a River" by his senior class. They couldn't quite understand his fondness for collard greens, chewing tobacco, and stock car racing but wrote it off as a consequence of that river water in his ears as a baby.

After graduating from Harvard, he returned to take his place in the family business as a junior executive-in-training. He walked around the plant in his fine three-piece suit, took notes on a clipboard, and mentioned to anyone who might not know, that his last name was Roe. He participated in board meetings where high level decisions were made regarding future pay cuts and longer hours for the employees. By all appearances, he was on his way to being the next chairman of the board.

But he just could not shake the Redneck raisin' that his real mama had instilled in him. He tried his best to be Figa in every way, but ever so often (like when he heard country music), *Moose* would break through and he could not control the urge to have a bowl of grits or chew a little Red Man. This would prove to be his undoing with the Roe family.

One day as he strolled through the plant, he came upon one of the Yankee supervisors giving a poor ol'

Redneck down the road. The supervisor was hollerin', cussin', kickin' dirt on the fellow's bare feet, and it sounded like he even said something ugly about the ol' boy's mama. There was nothing the Redneck could do but stand there and take it. He had hungry mouths to feed at home and was in debt to the company up to the bib of his overalls. There was nothing Figa could do, but this was more than he could stand. So he turned the *Moose* aloose. He grabbed that supervisor by the scruff of the neck, picked him slam up off the floor, and began to explain the new company benefit of on-the-job gall bladder removal, and would he like to have his done now. He dragged that fellow up one side of the plant and back down the other. He kicked that man's butt until he wore the top off his executive wing tips and then kept kicking with his bare foot.

When he thought that he had made his point and finally turned the subject of his animosity loose, that supervisor tore out like a scalded dog and didn't stop running until he had at least three counties between him and whatever had just given him the butt whuppin' of a lifetime.

As Moose calmed down, he began to realize that his life would never be the same again. He thought that he had checked around to see that no one was watching before starting that little tussle, but he was wrong. He could see that little bald-headed, weasle-faced step-cousin, grinning from ear to ear and heading toward granddaddy's office. He knew that no matter how much he liked Figa, Mr. Ze would not tolerate his beating the stuffing out of one of his supervisors—especially in front of the lowly Rednecks. He would probably put Moose in jail, or worse, send him back to Harvard for more "gentleman" training.

Moose didn't even go back up to the big house to say good-bye to his adopted mother. Anyway, she was probably off at the Junior League meeting or down at the river still flirting with sailors. He went straight to Mama's house, told her what he had done, and that he was on his way out of town. First thing Mama did, while trying her best to keep a straight face, was to scold Moose for fighting. Then she packed him a lunch of side meat, some left over sweet 'taters, and several cold biscuits for the trip. Since Moose did not know exactly where he was going, she suggested he head for West Virginia and look up her brother who might give him a place to stay for a while. He kissed Mama good-bye and, stealing a line from a future general, vowed, "I shall return."

Getting to West Virginia proved to be a lot harder than Moose had anticipated. He somehow took a wrong turn coming out of Newark on the New Jersey Turnpike and wound up square in the middle of downtown Brooklyn. It didn't take him long to figure out that this was no place for a fellow who had recently dedicated his life to being a full-time Redneck.

Finally straightened out and headed south, he made pretty good time all the way to Philadelphia where his progress was slowed considerably by all the heavy traffic downtown. A bunch of irate taxpayers had come to see some new bell that had cracked the first time they tried to ring it—even in those days government projects went to the lowest bidder. Moose took the liberty of skipping the bell debacle and boldly bolted beyond the burgeoning bourgeoisie. (Very good! With a

little practice we should soon be ready to try the more advanced *Peter Piper* alliteration.)

A couple of days later, he arrived at a town known as the District of Columbia. He was slam out of food, tired, sleepy, and his feet were killing him. All he wanted to do was keep right on moving and be on the other side before dark, but it was a strange city. Even though everybody seemed to be moving in a hurry, they never got anywhere or got anything accomplished. First he got tangled up with a group of Japanese tourists and was pushed and shoved into a tour of the Lincoln Memorial. This was made even more frustrating because nobody could figure out why a monument had been built to a man who would not even be born for several more centuries. Then he got hung up with another crowd a few blocks away where some nut was making false teeth from cherry trees and trying to throw them across a river (the Indians called this practice "Potomac," meaning "pale face with brain of muskrat"). Worse than that, this nut kept going on about how someday the city would be named after him, and he wanted everyone to call him the father of his country. Finally Moose broke free just outside the beltway and made a mental note that this would be a great place for a landfill, not knowing, of course, how the future would prove him correct.

After several more days of trudging through East Virginia, he came to a sign that read "Welcome to North Carolina" and made a mental note to get a new compass. He turned back to the north and west and finally intercepted the Appalachian Trail where he was promptly trampled by several hundred hikers who had just finished college and thought that walking from Georgia to Maine with a heavy pack on your back was better than getting an actual job.

Moose was tired. I am tired. You must be exhausted. Through the miracle of advanced typing technology, Moose finally arrived at the home of his Uncle Jethro. After living with his Uncle Jed in Beverly Hills and enjoying a successful career as a brain surgeon or short order cook—he couldn't remember which—Jethro had returned to West Virginia a number of years before. He had, however, managed to save enough money to buy a considerable amount of land and was now a successful farmer and/or moonshiner—it was really difficult to tell the difference.

Deciding that it would be best to stay away from the moonshine, except for the occasional cold, Moose started helping his uncle with the farming end of the business.

He plowed the fields, planted corn and barley, and taught his favorite mule tricks, such as standing on his hind legs and doing an impersonation of Uncle Jethro. The mule could not maintain this upright position for very long at one time, but then, neither could Uncle Jethro.

The country life was good and Moose grew to love it. "Early to bed, early to rise, the women are ugly, but so are the guys." Overalls suited him much better than a three-piece suit, and he had never liked wing tips. Figa was gone and all remnants of the Roe family traits were wiped away. He had become a full Redneck residing in the tribe of Hillbilly. His mind was clear and the hard work had made him more physically fit than he had ever been—except for the rather frequent bad colds which required ample medication.

It was about time for Moose to start looking for a mate. There were not a whole lot of ladies to choose from, but Uncle Jethro did have one daughter who had been giving Moose the eye. She was really nice looking after several doses of cold medicine and met all the other requirements of being able to cook, clean, perform small engine repair, and whittle stupid little mountain toys to sell to the Yankee tourists. Even more importantly, she was a first cousin. So Moose and Zippo were married and, as was the custom, moved into a nice double-wide parked in Jethro's backyard. Moose continued his farming chores while his wife took up a new hobby of making cigarette lighters. Soon, along came a bouncing (this practice has since been determined to be detrimental to most children) baby boy who was his father's spitting image . . . literally. He spit on the floor, he spit on his parents, he spit on the livestock. This kid was a spitting machine, so they named him Gus, which means "Gus."

CHAPTER XI

L . . . L . . . Let
M . . . M . . . My
P . . . P . . . P . . . People Go

everal years later Moose was plowing a field of corn way out in the back forty when he saw a bright light in the woods just over the ridge. Fearing that one of his father-in-law's stills had exploded, he dropped the plow and took off toward the light. As he topped the ridge, he could tell that it was only a chinaberry tree on fire, and even though it was covered in flames, it wasn't being burned. This might be worth a closer look. Drawing nearer, he heard a commanding voice speaking to him from inside the burning tree. Remembering back to stories that he had heard about his forefathers, he immediately recognized the voice as belonging to James Earl Jones.

The voice spoke again and told him that it was in fact God, not Mr. Jones. Moose's mama had told him a lot about God, but she had never mentioned anything about burning trees or booming voices. God was used to this kind of reaction by now and knew that He would have to take the time to prove to Moose that it was really Him.

"Lay your staff on the ground," commanded God. Moose dropped the stick and it immediately turned into the largest, longest snake that he had ever seen. (Note: A staff at this time was a sturdy stick used by people for walking around in the woods. It was somewhat unusual for it to turn into a snake. Today, on the other hand, a staff is a group of people who assist and advise a high-ranking official, such as a president. It is not unusual for these people to turn into snakes.)

Looking at this snake, Moose remembered something he'd been told about his original foreperson, Adam, and took off down the hill at top speed. God had anticipated this, grabbed Moose by the straps of his overalls, and pulled him back to the tree.

"Pick up the snake by the tail," God directed. Moose really wanted to, but his brain just couldn't convince his hand that it was such a good idea. God was beginning to tire of this little exercise and flung the snake into Moose's hand whereupon it turned back into a stick. Although somewhat still shaken, as evidenced by his desperate need for a change of overalls, Moose was convinced.

"Moose, I have a little job for you," God continued. "My people have suffered long enough in the Hinterlands. They have hopefully learned their lesson and are ready to return to Me. I want you to go back to New Jersey and lead them back to the Promised Land." Moose thanked Him for His kind offer but allowed as to how he was really pretty happy where he was, and it might be better if He found somebody else. God had to explain once again about how He was in charge; He had picked the man He wanted; and if it were necessary, He could do the snake number *one more time*. Snakes are a powerful motivator—Moose agreed.

But he still couldn't imagine how the Roe family would release all these people from their debts, and if they did, why would the Rednecks follow him? God told him not to worry; He had everything worked out. He had a few tricks up His sleeve to convince the Roes and besides, he could take the snake/staff as a sign of his authority. Moose was unable to persuade God to let him take the burning bush instead of the snake.

Zippo was not real sure that Moose hadn't been overindulging in the cold medicine, but like a dutiful wife (no really, there was a time when they were like that) she packed their belongings (everything except that soiled pair of overalls) and prepared for the trip to New Jersey. Jethro was even more skeptical and kept trying to get Moose to turn the stick into a snake or at least show him the chinaberry tree. Jethro had always been real fond of Moose, and when he couldn't convince him not to go, he gave him his favorite mule to make the trip. Besides, he was durn tired of that mule's imitation of him.

Moose, Zippo, and Gus left West Virginia with a heavy heart and two gallons of cold medicine. One thing for sure, on the way north they would take a different route, which did not include the District of Columbia or

Philadelphia. Two weeks later they arrived in New Jersey and rushed to meet with the family that he had left many years ago. Moose could not wait to tell them about how he had come to set them free and lead them back to the Promised Land. They looked at him like he was still wearing that pair of overalls he messed up at the burning tree. It was time for the snake. He threw the staff down in front of them, and sure enough, it turned into a snake. Remember, we are dealing with a group of purebred Rednecks here. It took several hours to find all those folks and get them back to where he could finish telling them all the good news. It all sounded real good, but these folks had been going through hard times for quite a while and weren't too sure that the "Big Boss" was going to let them go.

The next morning, bright and early, Moose headed off to the Roe headquarters. He marched right past all the security and office personnel directly to the office of the president. When he swung the door open, who should he find sitting behind the desk but his bald-headed, weasel-faced ex-step-cousin, Fay Roe. (Had you already guessed this by now? I promise this is the last Roe.) Fay stood there in his three-piece, custom-tailored (except for the unexplained wedgie that had just developed) Armani suit. The president of the vast Roe empire was sneering at his ex-step-cousin who was dressed in a pair of worn-out overalls and apparently working for a company that sold large sticks.

"To what do I owe this pleasure?" asked Fay in his most arrogant tone.

Moose summoned all his courage and replied "Bbbbbb gggg, pppp, ffff, ttttt!" What a time for his old stuttering problem to resurface. By the time he finally got out what he wanted to say, most of the Rednecks would already be dead. (Not a chance. God was well aware of the stuttering problem, and Plan B was set in motion.) At that exact moment, Moose's brother Arnold came through the door. After a short conference, they agreed that Moose would talk to God, and Arnold would talk to everybody else.

Arnold began in his most eloquent Southern business drawl, "Good morning, Mr. Roe. My name is Arnold and I'll be speaking on behalf of my brother for the next few minutes. Thank you for having us in your office. Let my people go!"

Fay could contain himself no longer, and through fits of laughter, managed to blurt out, "Why should I let your people go, and can you get Moose to do that stuttering thing again?"

Arnold held a quick sidebar conference with Moose and replied "Let the people go because God said so. As for the stuttering thing, Moose would rather not, but he will be glad to do a little tap dance on that bald dome of yours."

Even though it had been years ago, Fay still remembered the Olympic-class butt whuppin' Moose had put on that supervisor, so in the interest of keeping his head free of scuff marks, he dropped the fun making. But Roe Industries had come to rely on the poverty wages and long hours of the lowly Rednecks to fatten its bottom line. No way he was going to give them up easily. "How do I know that God wants these people to leave?" asked Fay. "How can you prove to me that you are a messenger from God?"

Moose told Arnold about the staff and when he threw it on the ground, sure enough it turned into a snake. "Cool!" said Arnold. Arnold had, through years of intense therapy, overcome the customary Redneck fear of snakes.

Fay, on the other hand, was not nearly so impressed. He called in his executive staff, and as was alluded to earlier, they also turned into snakes. Arnold argued that this was not really a miracle because they still had arms and legs, but there was no denying they were a bunch of vipers. Fay was late for a board meeting, so they scheduled an appointment for ten the next morning to divulge God's plagues. They declined Fay's further offer to "do lunch."

That night, Moose spent a lot of time with God getting the game plan down. It involved several steps, and Moose didn't want to get them out of order. He also got to spend a little time with his Mama and eat several dozen of her home-made biscuits. He was still belching flour rings when he finally dozed off to sleep.

The next morning at ten sharp, Moose and Arnold were back in Fay Roe's office. "Let my people go," repeated Arnold, "or God will cause your business to fall on hard times."

"Just how will He do that?" Fay sneered.

Arnold held out Moose's stick and touched a copy of the *Wall Street Journal*. When Fay picked it up and read the stock quotes, he saw that the price of bricks had gone through the floor. Roe Industries would be ruined because this was their only product. But Fay didn't get to be president only because he was a Roe (yes, he did). He looked straight at his two nemeses and declared, "No problem! If the price of bricks is now half as much, we will just make twice as many. Your people can thank you for the opportunity to work twice as hard and twice as long for half the money."

Moose figured he must have missed some part of God's plan. This really wasn't what he expected. He and Arnold excused themselves between Roe executive guffaws and asked to be penciled in once again for ten o'clock the following morning. As they walked out the front door, they were met by a group of Rednecks who had already gotten the word about the longer hours and less pay. This group did not fit into the *happy camper* category. They suggested that Moose might be a lot happier, or at least a lot more alive, if he were to return to West Virginia. They really didn't think they could stand any more of his *freeing them from oppression.*

That night Moose had some real serious conversation with God. This time he had a pad and pencil, tape recorder, and Arnold to make sure he was getting this stuff right. God assured him that even what seemed like a disaster today, was all in the Plan. He wanted Fay Roe to get overconfident and let his arrogance bring him down. Moose made a note about "pride goeth before a fall," and thought it might come in handy if he ever wrote a book.

Expecting another good laugh, the next morning Fay and his boys were anxiously awaiting the arrival of Abbott and Costello. Their sides were still hurting from all the laughing at yesterday's meeting.

Arnold began as usual, "Let my people go!"

"Or what?" Fay played the straight man.

Momentarily forgetting about the stuttering problem, Moose blurted out "Bbbbbb gggg, pppp, ffff, ttttt!" It took several minutes for the meeting to come back to order.

Arnold touched the morning paper with the staff and told Fay to read the headlines. In big bold letters on the front page, **Stucco Replaces Brick As Favorite Building Material.** There was no laughter this time. This was serious. They had enough bricks from all the overtime to last forty forevers. But Fay was not about to give in. All workers would be laid off until the factories were converted to produce stucco. This boy was not going to be easy to deal with, but God had promised to free His people and had a whole arsenal of little unpleasantries to bring Fay Roe to the same conclusion.

The next day Moose sat on top of the tallest building in town and blew non-stop on a special whistle. It had a very high pitch that only Yankees could hear and sounded exactly like Roseanne screeching out the National Anthem. But because he was adopted, Moose did not know that the entire Roe family was tone deaf and this had no effect whatsoever.

For His next number, God made the rivers and all drinking water taste like Thunderbird wine with a dead possum floating in it. After that came the plague of the gnats. This was no problem for the Rednecks who were well trained in the "blow out one side of your mouth and eat on the other side" procedure. Yankees, on the other hand, were continually swatting with both hands, swallowing mouthfuls of gnats, and worst of all, breathing them up their noses. Swat, gag, sneeze; swat, gag, sneeze; they were beginning to soften, but still would not let the people go.

No more Mr. Nice Guy. The gloves came off for the next plague. Everything the Yankees cooked smelled like cabbage and tasted like airline food. Fay Roe was on the verge of sending for Moose, but his pride and greed won out over the bad taste in his mouth and the ring around his rear from long hours of sitting on the porcelain throne.

When God told him about the last plague, Moose thought it was too cruel and inhumane even for Yankees. But God assured him that this one would do it and then they could be on their way home. For the next week, the only thing on television was reruns of *The Beverly Hillbillies*. People were rioting in the streets. Some became so desperate that they even went to the library and checked out classical literature. Even Fay Roe finally realized that this was more than could be humanly tolerated and sent for Moose.

"Your people are free to go," conceded Fay. "And go quickly, before we miss another episode of *Gilligan's Island*."

CHAPTER XII

Are We There Yet?

t had worked just as God had said it would. Fay Roe had not only wiped the books clean of all their debts, but also had thrown in two weeks' severance pay and given everybody a company T-shirt. The Rednecks were free to return to the Promised Land.

Moving that many people seven or eight hundred miles south was not an easy task. It was a logistical nightmare, even if everything went according to plan. It would have been even worse unless Moose did, in fact, come up with a plan to go according to. This was a really good time to hold a board meeting with God to work out some of these minor details.

"OK Listen up!" Arnold shouted at the assembled mass of Redneck humanity. "We will be leaving Thursday morning at 10:00 A.M. sharp. Everyone is allowed one checked bag not to exceed sixty-two inches in circumference and one carry-on that will fit easily on your own back. Seating assignments will not be necessary since we will be walking."

At the appointed time, Moose held high his staff and started boldly off in the direction of Brooklyn. Fortunately, Arnold was a much better navigator and steered him back on course toward I-95 south. The people followed while triumphantly singing that old classic spiritual "On the Road Again" by Willie Nelson and littering the roadside with beverage cans and candy wrappers.

For such a large crowd of people and in spite of the holiday traffic, they were actually making pretty good time. With all the adults, children, and bags crammed together; the continual bathroom stops at every rest area; "Are we there yet?" ringing constantly in every ear; Billy Ray's looking at me funny!" and "I will stop this walk right this instant

and wear your fanny out!" and several dogs throwing up in the exact location of future station wagon back seats, this was pretty much your ordinary family vacation trip.

Emboldened by his success to this point, Moose headed straight for the District of Columbia. With the crowd he had behind him, he was bound to outnumber almost everyone else, except maybe the lobbyists. Rush hour in D.C. is not to be trifled with. Every bridge leading out of the city was clogged with traffic and there was no way they were going to be able to get out of town before dark. Moose was determined not to spend the night there because their per diem would not begin to cover hotel costs, never mind a decent meal.

Just as it looked as though they might have to bed down for the evening on a heated grate along Pennsylvania Avenue, God showed them another way out. As per His direction, Moose held his staff out over the waters of the Potomac. The waters instantly parted, and the Rednecks crossed to the Virginia side on dry ground. Just as Moose was about to let the waters fill the space, he was approached by a young man wearing a white wig. The young man, who looked vaguely familiar, asked if Moose would mind holding the water back just a while longer so that he could re-trieve several sets of wooden false teeth that he had stupidly thrown into the river several years ago. As this man was finishing picking up his teeth, along with quite a few sil-ver dollars, Moose noticed a group of well-dressed men entering the dry river bed from the other side. It seemed as though Fay Roe had had a change of heart about letting his employees go, and the company legal department had found a loop-hole in the Plague and Release Agreement. It is not too difficult to recognize men wearing three-piece business suits, carrying briefcases, and waving papers over their heads as attorneys, even if there is not an ambulance in front of them at the time. Suddenly Moose's arms grew tired (har, har), and he could no longer hold them up above the river. It was a horrible sight to see. As the waters covered the lawyers, the poor fish and other river inhabitants tried valiantly to clamber up the muddy banks and out of the polluted water.

Once the people had escaped the congestion of D.C. and emerged on the south side of the beltway, it was clear sailing through southern Virginia all the way into Kentucky. Moose pushed the people hard to put as much distance as possible be-tween them and New Jersey. Not until they had crossed through the Cumberland Gap into Tennessee was he able to relax and consider giving the people a rest. Even then he continued on several days past Knoxville, and not until he reached Gatlinburg did he tell the people that they could remain there for a time to rest up and regroup. This was an ideal place to stop. It had beautiful scenery, tons of antique and gift shops, and Pigeon Forge and Dollywood were only about an hour away.

Moose soon found out that people with tired feet can be difficult to deal with. They started complaining about being thirsty and not having anything to drink. God instructed Moose to strike a certain rock with his staff. Moose inquired as to whether it would turn into a

snake again, and if so, he would let Arnold do the rock striking. God assured him that it would not, and when he struck the rock it flowed with original, diet, and caffeine-free Coke. There was still some grumbling from a few who wanted mineral water, ginger ale, Gatorade, or a selection of herb teas, but Moose wasn't about to bother God with that.

Next thing you know, they were hungry and there was nothing to eat. Perish the thought that they might have to fix something for themselves. The teenage mentality was running rampant through this crowd. Once again, God showed His caring nature by providing for their needs. Every morning when they woke, they found sitting on the table in the kitchenette a steaming bowl of grits and red-eye gravy. To honor Him who had provided sustenance, the people called this meal "manna," which means "God is not only Sovereign but also Southern."

Too much leisure time can sometimes become a problem for people who have never had any. (Obviously, it did here or I would not have mentioned it. I am a trained writing professional.) They spent endless hours riding cable cars, attending authentic Wild West show gunfights, and playing arcade video games until their brains turned into seven and three-quarters pounds of mush. Credit cards were filled to overflowing with purchases of antiques and genuine, hand-whittled, mountain folk arts and games. When asked about the "Made in Taiwan" stickers on the bottom, the locals were able to convince these morons that Taiwan was Appalachian for "the dark," because all their work was done at night.

Moose could see that these people needed some guidelines to help them through life. God agreed and told Moose that He would meet with him in a week on top of the mountain and they would hammer out a few rules. On the appointed day the temperature was in the mid-sixties, the barometer was rising, and the stock market was up in moderate trading. The skies were clear, except for the top of the mountain, which was covered by a dark cloud streaked with lightning and booming with thunder. Although, as previously mentioned, they were not exceptionally gifted mentally, the Rednecks rapidly deduced that this was a good day to stay off the sky buckets going up the mountain. Moose knew that it might take a few days to complete his business with God and assigned Arnold the job of interim Head-Most Preacher until he got back. He then put on his most comfortable pair of Timberland hiking boots and started up the hill.

Arnold had been a capable mouthpiece for Moose, but this was his first chance to be totally in charge. The power was nice, but these people could really be a handful. They were constantly griping about everything, and he couldn't get them to go to church, except when they had dinner on the ground. They had been up north so long that they could only worship things they could see. A mountain with flashing lightning and booming thunder would seem to have been enough but not for these people.

They kept bugging Arnold, and finally under the threat of bodily harm, he agreed to fashion an idol from various jewelry and trinkets. Using all his skill and artistry, Arnold managed to make something that resembled a '57 Chevy with the hood up and passenger side door open. With all its unhallowed hideousness, it was exactly what the people wanted. They immediately ordered several kegs, broke out some chips and dip, and lined up a dance band.

Up on the mountain, God and Moose had come up with about 350 principles intended to help the people get their act together, but they also knew that there was no way these clowns could remember more than about a dozen or so. Finally they narrowed it down to fifteen that ought to do it. Moose was exhausted and took a nap while God wrote the rules down on a couple of stones.

Talk about your bad timing. Moose came down from the moun-

tain top just as the party was getting into full swing. To say he was displeased would be like saying the U.S. was peeved at Japan about Pearl Harbor (of course, no one would have said this at that time). He raised the stone tablets containing the rules above his head and with all his might threw them down on the front seat of the '57 Chevy idol, causing all three tires to go flat (I told you it was hideous!). He then spent the next hour or so screaming and yelling at the people, kinda like when you come home with a report card containing a number of Ds and Fs (not that I would have a personal knowledge of how that must feel). Besides that, thanks to them he would now have to trudge back up the mountain and get more stone tablets and his feet were already killing him. While he was gone, they were to go to their rooms without supper, and they had better not make a sound until he got back! As for Arnold, he would deal with him later, much later, after he cooled off enough to stop imagining his brother's worthless carcass being dragged across the mountains behind that Chevy.

Several days later, Moose once again descended from the mountain with the tablets containing the fifteen rules. He assembled the people together and suggested they pay extremely close attention while he explained the new rules. The first ten were verbatim those in a previous Manuscript and needed no further explanation—except they better abide by them. There were five new ones that should help ease the transition from their life up north to their new life in the Promised Land.

XI Thou shalt not put sugar on thy grits.

XII Thou shalt not wear Bermuda shorts, sandals, and dark socks, ever.

XIII Thou shalt spend only the minimal time above the Mason-Dixon line required to accomplish thy task and then high-tail it back south.

XIV Thou shalt root only for SEC teams, no matter who they are playing in a bowl game.

XV Thou shalt not encourage Yankees to move south or thou wilt be vexed by their continual talking about how they did it up north.

They had rested in this place long enough, and now it was time to pack up and travel the last leg of their journey to the Promised Land. The Gatlinburgians begged them to remain a little longer until the few remaining antiques and trinkets had been purchased, but the Rednecks could barely load up what they had already bought. Besides, Moose was still angry about their past behavior and was not an easy man to reason with.

After several more days of exhausting travel through mountainous terrain, across rushing rivers, and along busy interstate highways, they arrived at a place called Chattanooga. According to Cherokee lore, it meant "Large Iron Horse Running on Rails and Belching Smoke." Due to the misbehaving in Gatlinburg, Moose put out strict orders that there would be no partying and no shopping. And he didn't care what the name meant—no riding on the Choo Choo!

Moose was getting up in years and this trip had taken a hard toll on him. Even though they were so close to the end of the journey, he knew that he would never set foot in the Promised Land. But God had pledged to him that he would be able to see it before he died. From the top of Lookout Mountain, Moose gazed longingly toward the South. It was a beautiful land of magnolia trees, camellia blossoms, mint julep, fields of cotton and peanuts, woods filled with deer, SEC football, and NASCAR races at the Talladega Speedway. It was the perfect place for the Rednecks. His work was done, and having seen the Promised Land, he could pass on a happy man.

Before going up on the mountain, Moose had chosen his successor to lead the people. It might have been Arnold, had it not been for the little goof-up in Gatlinburg. Arnold was missing one of the key ingredients that make a good leader—he couldn't get anybody to follow. But there was among the people a man who could carry the torch and lead the people home. Josh, from the tribe of Ua, was that man. He was an honorable man and had been a valuable assistant to Moose throughout the trip. Another advantage that Josh had was that the people *would* follow him.

When it became evident that Moose would not be coming down from the mountain, Josh Ua told the people to pack their stuff and prepare to cross over into the land which God had given them. As they crossed over the Tennessee border into Alabama, the Rednecks burst forth in songs, cheers, and more than a few distinct rebel yells. Even though none of these people had ever set foot on this ground before, they knew they were home—in the land of their ancestors—to stay.

CHAPTER XIII

Ya'll Need To Git On Back Up Yonder

ntering the Promised Land was one thing. Hanging on to it was going to be another. As usual, nothing came easy for these people. While so many of the Rednecks had been up north, a number of Yankee tribes had invaded the South and laid claim to various stretches of land. They had built cities from which they carried on their primary business practice—cheating the few poor Southerners left behind.

Josh and his followers had hardly traveled a day into the Promised Land when they ran right smack dab into one of these dens of iniquity. The city was called Jerry Coe and was occupied by a gang known as the Massachutians. It was surrounded by high walls made of leftover grits that these people could never learn to eat and kept throwing out their windows.

The Chosen People had just finished a long, hard journey. Their feet were killing them, and they just

really didn't want to go picking a fight, even if they were Yankees. Josh knew that they would have to deal with this situation sooner or later, so they might as well deal with it sooner. Besides, God suggested it would be a good time and Moose had really emphasized to Josh the importance of following God's advice because He could do that snake thing in a New York second.

Adhering to the plan that God had laid out, they marched around and around the city for seven days straight. Now, not only were their feet hurting, but they were getting dizzy from walking in circles. On the seventh day, when the sun was high in the sky and the temperature was in the mid-nineties, God sent down large boulders of butter onto the walls. As the butter melted and mixed with the grits, the walls started to flow down the hillside. The Rednecks rushed the walls, sprinkled on a little salt and pepper, and sat down for a feast. Finally, when they had eaten their fill, Josh was able to get them moving again, and they proceeded to whup some northern butt. The Massachutians didn't like wearing grits any better than they liked eating them and ran out of the "baas" (saloons), jumped in their paaked "caas" (in this case, it would have been wagons in the pre-car era, but they don't say wagon funny), and tore out for "Baaston" (a northern city where everyone wears red sox and eats beans).

Centuries later, Jerry Coe was again taken over by the Massachutians. This time they were wearing MIT sweaters and were accompanied by a number of German scientists. They changed the name of the city to Huntsville and used it as a base to play with rockets. But since they also brought lots of money and jobs with them, they were welcomed with open arms.

It would be nice if this took care of the Yankee plague, but no such luck. Scattered throughout the Promised Land were numerous other clans that would continue to pester the Rednecks for years to come. There were the Indianaites, the Chicagonians, and the Michiganians from way up north. Another group, the Minnesotians, had pretty much become extinct by now because their entire existence was based on snow. From Ohio came the Buckites and from Maryland the Baltimites. Also from the far reaches of south Florida came the mutant offspring of snowbirds known as the Miamians. And the most bothersome bunch of all, who continually stayed in the faces of the Rednecks were the Phillystines.

The Yankees would have to wait. The first order of business was to divide the land and make sure each family had forty acres and a mule. Since there were two main clans of Rednecks, Josh decided it best to split the state down the middle and give half to each one. The Tuscaloosians got the western half and were to dress in crimson and white. The Auburnites got the eastern half and were to dress in orange and blue. According to the rules, they were supposed to meet only once each year and must adhere strictly to the dress code to minimize any chance of their offspring intermarrying. The dress code would also come in handy when one had entirely too much elixir and couldn't exactly remember to which side one belonged.

At this annual gathering, the clans were encouraged to yell things at each other, such as "Roll Tide" and "War Eagle," and then spend the next several hours trying to figure out what the heck they meant. Sometimes as an added attraction there would be a sporting event played during half-time to give a short break to the *yellers*. For the remainder of the year, the winners of this event could enjoy a pastime called "rubbing it in" by calling out the score every time they saw someone from the opposing clan. The losing clan was obliged by its *dregs of humanity* status to respond with "wait until next year."

It was during one of these get-togethers that the great leader Josh met his demise. It was the fourth quarter with two seconds to go. The score was tied. The teams lined up for a forty-yard field goal. As the ball was kicked, the crowd came to its feet. Josh was unable to see from his nosebleed location in Section 102, Row 60, Seat 27 (not even

Josh could get good seats to this game). He stood up on the top wall to get a better view and lost his balance when he was hit in the face by one of those annoying pom-pom, shaker things. Fortunately, at the age of 110 he died of natural causes on the way down, despite prompt medical attention several hours later after the stadium had cleared and traffic had died down.

With the confusion surrounding Josh's fall, the referee had failed to watch the field goal, and the game was declared a tie. Things were quiet the next year because neither side knew what to yell in case of a draw. Of lesser significance, but still important, Josh had failed to name a successor to lead the people. Since the game was a tie, they couldn't simply let the Most Valuable Player assume leadership. So they just decided to go home and press on without a

leader. Knowing this group, that spelled T-R-O-U-B-L-E (for those of you who don't spell very well, it's trouble).

There were still a lot of alien Yankee life forms lurking around the land. One group, the Indianaites, began to stir up a lot of trouble. They were always asking the same annoying questions over and over and over again. "Who's your friend?" "Who's your buddy?" "Who's your pal?" They did this to the point that they finally became known as the "Who's Yours." Enough is enough. The Rednecks needed a leader to get rid of these pests once and for all.

As usual, God had a man for the job. He picked Gerald, a common man who made his living selling vegetables from a roadside stand in front of his trailer. It was rumored that he had once grown a rutabaga the size of a hubcap, but since cars

were still not yet invented, there was no way to prove it. Gerald, however, had a slightly higher IQ than the rutabaga and wanted proof that this was really God speaking to him before he got into some kind of tussle with the Indianaites.

He said to God, "I will leave my long johns outside tonight. If, in the morning, they are wet with dew and the ground is dry, I will know that it is You." The next morning, sure enough, the long johns were soaking wet and the ground was as dry as a powder house. But Gerald was still reluctant to lead a bunch of Rednecks into a fracas. Besides that, he had several large dogs around the house that wouldn't be above hosing down a piece of his clothing just for fun. To make sure, he asked God to do the same thing once more, but this time in reverse. The next morning, the ground was soaked with dew all the way to Mississippi, and his long johns were dry as a bone. He couldn't stall any longer.

Leaving his oldest boy in charge of the vegetable stand, he set out to put together a big enough group to run off the Indianaites. These Who's Yours had been so obnoxious that pretty soon he had a slew of folks who were sick and tired of their stupid questions and ready to drive them back up north. But God thought Gerald had too many men. "Tell all the men to turn back who have been wearing the same under-drawers for more than a week," God suggested. Two-thirds of them were gone in a flash and those remaining noticed an immediate improvement in the air quality.

"You still have too many men," God continued. "Watch them when they drink water. Those that lap water from the stream like a dog, send home. Those that get tickled and spew water out their noses, send home. Those who stay under too long and almost drown, send to 'I am not a fish' therapy."

He would need only those men who were smart enough to use the plainly-marked-strategically-located-in-an-obvious-place-in-the-middle-of-the-campground water fountain. This left about three hundred men, and God told Gerald this was just the right number.

God's plan was fairly simple (whew!). Each man was issued a trumpet and a basket. Under cover of darkness, Gerald and the boys took to the hills surrounding the Indianaite town. When Gerald gave the signal, each man dumped his basket, which contained a ball (this, of course, is where we get basketball), and began to play the University of Indiana Fight Song. With all the basketballs rolling down the hills into the streets and the sound of the music ringing in their ears, the Who's Yours had to play some hoops. Only one problem. There were no goals or backboards in the South. They would have to go all the way back to Indiana to find some. Sure, there were goals in Kentucky, but they were all in use. Within the hour the whole bunch of them had dribbled north, and the problem was solved.

God continued to use various leaders and methods to rid the South of these unwanted invaders. Rumors of impending colder weather and the possibility of a lottery sent the Miamians scurrying back to south Florida. The Buckites and Michiganians packed up when told that the winner of a contest back home would receive a trip to the Rose Bowl. The Baltimites left willingly when the Orioles made the World Series, and the Chicagonians pulled out when they realized how much they missed "da' Bears and da' Bulls." There was one group left who was going to continue to be a thorn in the Redneck side for some time to come—the Phillystines.

CHAPTER XIV

Hoss And
The Phillystines

he Phillystines had come pouring into the South some years ago due, primarily, to a tax-payer revolt over some cracked bell incident. They had settled mostly around the Dothan area and were making a fortune in the peanut business. With this money, they had diversified into banking and con-struction and controlled most of the money and jobs in the region. They viewed with contempt the native Redneck practice of boiling peanuts and would only allow roasted ones at ball games. Once again the Cho-sen People were being treated like yard dogs in their own land.

But as usual, God noticed their suffering and took pity on them. He had just the person in mind to bring a little rain on the Phillystine parade. Some years before, He had anticipated this situation and had blessed a barren couple with a very special baby. The grateful parents were instructed to never cut the child's sideburns. His name was (no, not Elvis) Sam. He grew to be a strapping young fellow who towered above all the other boys his age. Of course, he had started out big, weighing over fifteen pounds at birth. When his mama "came to" several months later, she knew he was going to be exceptional. Sam continued to grow so rapidly in stature and in strength that before he was ten years old, he had already acquired a descriptive nickname that would follow him throughout life—everybody called him "Hoss."

Hoss was a little on the mean side and quite a fighter. This was probably due to all the teasing he had taken in elementary and junior high school because of the sideburns. He went on to finish school and even played football at Auburn under the name of Bo Jackson and at Alabama under the name of Joe Namath—in the same game. He also seemed to be born with a nat-ural dislike for the Phillystines. Anytime he caught less than several dozen of them alone, he immediately started a butt whuppin' party, and they were the door prizes. This got to be embarrassing, not to mention painful, to the Phillystines, so they decided it was time they arrested this menace and locked him up for a while.

The local sheriff got up a posse of several hundred men and set out to bring Hoss to "justice." Around noon the next day, they found him sitting under a shade tree where he was enjoying his usual lunch of cornbread and collards. When the sheriff explained why they had come, Hoss explained how that wasn't going to happen, and they might just as well get on with the scuffle. He grabbed the first thing he could get his hands on, which happened to be the jawbone of a donkey. When he started swinging that thing, members of the posse were flying in all directions. As disconcerting as this was to the Phillystines, it was even worse on the donkey, who, as luck would have it, was still attached to his jawbone. In one of only a few such recorded incidents in history, the donkey quickly mastered the art of speech and suggested to Hoss that a two-by-four or sturdy limb might make an equally effective weapon. When Hoss let him go, the donkey, followed closely by the Phillystine posse, tore out for the barn.

Since logic, reason, and several hundred heavily armed men had not worked with Hoss, the Phillystines decided to resort to the more covert and less painful strategy of deception. There must be some secret besides cornbread and collards to a man's being that strong. One sure way to get most men to spill their guts is through a good looking woman. The Phillystines just happened to know one, who was of the serious female persuasion. Her name was Della. I'm talking about a fine looking woman! She would be perfect for this little job. Not only was she beautiful outside, but inside she had the heart of a psychotic loan officer. For the correct currency, there was no doubt that she would deliver Hoss into their hands.

They made sure that she just happened to be at all the same places Hoss frequented. Wherever Hoss went, Della was there in her most provocative outfit and enough makeup to paint a Wal-Mart. Sure enough, one day he spotted her across a crowded stockyard at the weekly donkey auction. He was so spellbound by her looks that he started braying like a jackass and the bid was up to $400 before the auctioneer realized that he was mostly human. Even though God and his mama had warned him not to hang around Phillystine women, Hoss just couldn't help himself. He sauntered out across the middle of the stockyard floor and slung burros Hither and Yon (since Hither was a much smaller burro, he was thrown about twenty yards further than Yon). Hoss climbed the stairs to where Della was sitting, eased up next to her, and asked if she would like to go to the picture show on Saturday night. She told him no, because there was no such thing as a picture show yet; however, he could come over to her house and sit on the front porch swing if he promised not to do that stupid braying again.

Saturday night came, and Hoss went over to Della's. They sat in the swing, looked at the stars, and nibbled on possum hors d'oeuvres. Della began her deception by flattering Hoss about his uncommon strength.

"Oh, Hoss, you have just got the biggest ol' muscles I have ever seen," Della cooed. "What in the world makes you so strong?"

"It's a secret," Hoss mumbled through a mouthful of possum. "God and mama don't want me telling nobody."

"But I'm not just anybody, Hoss," Della persisted. "I thought that I was your special girl." Boy, it was hard to deny somebody that looked and smelled so good.

"Okay, I'll tell you," Hoss gave in. "If you tie my hands behind my back with the shoe strings from a brand new pair of Nike Air Jordans, I won't be able to lift a finger."

Full of possum hors d'oeuvres, Hoss dozed off, and Della quickly ran down to the local sporting goods store and got a pair of the appropriate shoes (size 13EE). Hurriedly, before Hoss woke from his nap, she tied his hands tightly behind his back. Then she opened the door, yelled to the Phillystine men hiding out back, and woke up Hoss. Hoss popped those shoe strings like they weren't even there and commenced to put his usual whuppin' on the Phillystine men.

The next night, he was right back over at Della's house, and she started in on him. "You lied to me

and really hurt my feelings. Not to mention I'm out $110 for those durn shoes. No more smelling the perfume in my hair again until you tell me the truth."

This was tough because she was about the best smelling thing that Hoss had run up on since the chitlin' plant burned. "If I ever have my toenails painted a bright purple," Hoss declared in his most sincere voice, "I will turn into such a sissy that Richard Simmons will look like Hulk Hogan by comparison."

Della served him up another helping of everything on the table and filled his glass with more muscadine wine. As usual, the minute the last bite went into his mouth, Hoss dozed off. Della, as one might imagine, just happened to have a bottle of the brightest purple nail polish that Revlon made. She ripped off Hoss's boots, almost passed out, took a few minutes to catch her breath again, and started painting.

"Hoss! The Phillystines are coming," cried Della.

The Phillystine men stayed hidden this time because they wanted to make sure that Hoss was considerably weaker than the last go round. Hoss woke up, lisped a few S's, and asked where his exercise leotards were. Expecting to haul Hoss off in a dip net, the men rushed into the room. Just kidding! Hoss was such a big tease that he proceeded to stuff *all* those boys into *one* pair of leotards and leave them dangling out Della's window.

The next night Della was fit to be tied. Hoss could see by the pouty look on her face that there wasn't going to be any more perfume smelling or kissy-face until he told her the truth. Besides that, she had gotten to be a pretty good cook, and he sure did like to eat. "I'll tell you

the secret of my strength in a riddle," Hoss began.

**"I'll be too weak to get out of bed,
Without the hair on the
side of my head."**

(This boy had not only the strength of an ox, but an IQ to match.) Della had often wondered about his seven-foot sideburns, but had just figured he was so musclebound that he couldn't bend his arm enough to reach the side of his head. This must really be the secret!

She laid on some serious kissy-face and then cooked Hoss the best fried catfish he had ever put in his mouth. Several gallons of wine and several hundred hushpuppies later, he was into a major nap. Not wanting to take any chances this time, Della shaved Hoss from one end to the other. Then she covered his entire body with industrial-strength

Nair. Poor ol' Hoss didn't even have so much as a nose hair left on him.

"Hoss, the Phillystines are coming!" screamed Della. Hoss woke up but could hardly lift his head off the pillow. When the armed men came through the door, it was all he could do to wink and ask if they could come back later when he found his hair. They finally had their man and rushed him down to the county jail before somehow he got his strength back. Della sat counting her ill-gotten gains and wondering if all that food she fed Hoss could be deducted from her taxes as a business expense.

Hoss sat in his cell and chastised himself about how all this was his own fault. If only he had listened to God and Mama. Instead, he had listened to his stomach and allowed a woman to make a fool of him. As bad as things were, there was at least one bright spot. His

head was a whole lot cooler without those sideburns.

When the Phillystines were convinced that Hoss's strength was totally gone, they began to make him do menial chores around the courthouse in full view of everybody. He had to sweep the halls, clean the restrooms, empty the spittoons, and most embarrassing of all, he had to ride around the square on that three-wheel motorcycle checking parking meters and marking peoples' tires with baby-blue chalk. He knew he deserved it all but hoped someday he would have one last chance to get back at those boys.

It wasn't long before that chance came along. The Phillystines were holding their annual Charity Donkey Basketball Tournament to aid men maimed and disabled through earlier encounters with Hoss. They thought it would be funny to bring Hoss in and have him play the game blindfolded. The auditorium was packed to overflowing with all the Phillystine high-class snobs, all of whom were having a good laugh at poor old Hoss's expense. But this time, he would have the last laugh. One of the donkeys happened to be the same one that Hoss had grabbed by the jawbone several years before. When this particular animal recognized Hoss, it panicked and started braying and running all over the place. Of course, this spooked the rest of the two dozen or so donkeys and they stampeded up into the stands. By the time it was over, they had completely destroyed the entire building and there wasn't a Phillystine left standing, or one without at least a couple of hoof marks on his head. Reckon how that same donkey just happened to be there? I bet God and Mama know.

CHAPTER XV

Governors And
Other Goofups

ver since Josh passed away, the Rednecks had been wandering aimlessly with no real leader. God had raised up different people on an "as-needed" basis for trouble spots, but there was no full-time, recognized leader to keep them on the straight and narrow. So when they weren't fighting with Yankee vermin, they were fighting amongst themselves. Give them a couple of beers, and they would be rolling in the dirt over who had the ugliest horse or who's wife could run the fastest.

About the only person who came close to having any authority was an old preacher by the name of Earl, a direct descendant of Arnold, Moose's brother, who was the first designated Head-Most Preacher. But Earl was getting old. According to custom, he should have been passing the job on to one of his two boys, but they were entirely too worthless to take over his duties. In addition to stealing money out of the offering plate and guzzling all the ceremonial wine, they were chronic womanizers and had even been known to cheat at cards. One way or another they had everybody south of Nashville mad at them.

God, of course, had been aware of this little problem and had already hand-picked His next Head-Most Preacher. His name was Sam L. When he was just a little boy, his mama had promised him to God and sent him to live with Earl to learn preacher stuff. Sam L. was a dedicated young man and took to preaching like a duck to water.

Some years later, the wicked lifestyle—more specifically, two jealous husbands—finally caught up with Earl's boys. Earl was in the middle of dinner when he got the news and fell dead on the spot. Not so much from the shock of their passing as from the tater tot caught in his windpipe. Tater tots were rela-

tively new, and people did not know that some amount of chewing was required prior to swallowing.

This, of course, immediately projected Sam L. into the position of Head-Most Preacher. As with everything else, Sam L. took his new job seriously. Sam L. took everything seriously. Sam L. took the soap operas and wrestling seriously. Lighten up, Sam!

For many years, Sam L. provided guidance and counsel to his people. Life in the Promised Land was rocking along fairly well. The people were prospering, and both the Auburnites and Tuscaloosians were having one winning season after another. But eventually Sam L. began to get a little long in the tooth, and the Rednecks were concerned about his successor. He, like Earl, had two sons, but neither one of them was worth killing. (What is it with preachers' kids?). The people had no intention of letting these clowns replace Sam L., so they went and told him that they wanted a governor. Sam L. agreed about his sons but tried to tell them that having a governor might not be the shortest row in the field either. All the bureaucracy, capitol building, formal dinners, national guard, and highway patrol escorts were going to cost money. More money means higher taxes.

It didn't matter. All the other states had governors, and the Rednecks felt left out. They really, really, really wanted one, and if he didn't let them have one, they would lay down on the floor and hold their breath until they turned blue. The last thing that Sam L. wanted was a bunch of blue Rednecks, so he agreed to choose a governor for them. (Today we are fortunate to live in a democratic society where every citizen can participate in choosing our elected officials by going into a voting booth and selecting the most qualified candidates by repeatedly flipping a coin into the air.)

One thing that Sam L. had learned during preacher training was that you don't go making big decisions like this on your own. First thing he did was talk to God about who He thought would make a good governor. As usual, God was one step ahead and told Sam L. not to worry. He would send the right man to his house the next day. Sure enough, about noon the next day a man looking for some stray mules came by the church. He was a big ol' boy, clear of eye, and with arms like tree trunks. Sam L. got this tingling feeling all over and knew this was either the man that God had sent or his hives were acting up again. Just to make sure, he excused himself and went to pull up his robe to check for any red splotches. With none there he knew this must be the man.

Sam L. learned that the man's name was Billy Sol and he worked on his daddy's farm not far from town. They went next door to Harmon's Second Helping Café for the all-you-can-eat family style buffet. Sam L. started right in telling Billy Sol all about the plans for him to be the first governor. After Billy Sol had finished close to his twelfth helping of  fried okra, what Sam L. was talking about began to sink in. Billy Sol allowed as to how he was real honored to be asked, but he really had to find them mules right now. "Besides that," he asked, "what the heck is a governor and could you pass that fried okra just one more time?"

No-nonsense Sam L. told him not to worry about the mules because they were tied up behind the church. Then he explained, "A governor is a man who rules over people; makes laws; collects taxes; picks the state flower, bird, and song; defends the home folks from alien Yankee life forms—as well as from themselves; and no, there isn't any more okra. Besides that, God had picked you for the job and it would be a real bad idea to turn it down."

Since the mules were safe and the okra was gone, Billy Sol didn't have much else pressing right then and agreed to take the position. As was the custom, Sam L. anointed Billy Sol by pouring a quart of 10-30 over his head, but his hair was already so greasy it was difficult to tell the difference.

The first thing they had to do was get the word out to all the people and then invent something called an inauguration (literally, "big party at taxpayer expense"). Sam L.'s wife said she would take care of all the arrangements for the shindig and began lining up caterers and several dance bands. When the big day came, there were acres of gastronomical delights prepared by the premier chefs of the land. There was a table of boiled or fried and hand-slung, gourmet chitlins. Next to it was a washtub full of the finest pickled pig's feet you ever sunk a tooth into. There were catfish fingers, little cold collard sandwiches, watermelon slices, and a big bowl of pot likker in which to dip corn bread fritters. Of course, in honor of the new governor there was enough fried okra to cover three counties four feet deep.

As the band played "Stars Fell on Alabama," Sam L. administered the official oath of office to Billy Sol. It was met with a thunderous round of belching from the well-fed crowd. The Rednecks at last had a certified leader and the first Governor of Alabama. The dance bands were mostly a waste because everybody was too full to move, never mind dance. They just lay around rubbing their bellies wondering how often they could justify having an inauguration. This governor thing was going to be all right.

Billy Sol had not even finished brushing the crumbs off his overalls when the first crisis hit his administration. Word came to the capital that a bunch of the Miamians had crept back into south Alabama and were cheating the local folks out of everything they had. These Florida Yankees had started out innocently enough by setting up a couple of fresh fruit stands near the state line. Pretty soon that whole area was nothing but one fruit stand after another. And in addition to selling fruit at high prices, they were peddling all sorts of other trinkets, like coconut heads, stuffed alligators, and the most awful airbrushed T-shirts you've ever seen. The last straw was when they started reselling Florida lottery tickets at twice the price. Worst of all, they were last week's tickets.

Sam L. told the new governor that he had checked with God, and God said to go drive the intruders back to their own country. Billy Sol was to make sure that not only did he run off the people, but that they also took with them every piece of fruit, plus all the other junk that belonged to them. Nothing was to be left behind.

It took a couple of days to put together the Alabama National Guard. Then Billy Sol set out to face the Miamians. The Guard swooped down on the unsuspecting scoundrels like fruit flies and, in no time, had them in high gear headed back toward the land of sun, sand, and seashells. Then the Weekend Warriors went about tearing down all the fruit stands and the "Vine Ripe Tomatoes, 100 yards" signs along the road. The Redneck troops had destroyed just about everything in sight when

Billy Sol got a little curious and decided to try one of the tangerines. It was the first one he had ever seen and it tasted some more kind of good. He really didn't see any harm in keeping a couple dozen of them to eat around bedtime. And he just had to keep that one coconut head that was the spitting image of his loving wife, except for the large wart on the nose—his wife's, not the coconut's.

Being as how this was Billy Sol's first official act as governor, Sam L. thought it might be a good idea for him to check on this operation. When Sam L. rode up on his ministerial donkey, the first thing he saw was Billy Sol sitting there with tangerine juice running down the airbrushed swordfish on his new T-shirt and talking to that coconut head about how neat it was to be the "Guv". Serious Sam L. was not amused. God was especially not amused. Sam L. took what was left of the tangerines and squeezed them over Billy Sol's head and then the coconut head. He was very careful not to lick his fingers afterward.

Even though he had run off the Miamians, Billy Sol knew he was in deep trouble. He might be governor, but with Sam L. and God both mad at him life was going to be a real drag. Besides that, when he showed that look-alike coconut to his wife, she hit him upside his head with a pickled pig's foot left over from the inauguration.

CHAPTER XVI

The Crayon Is Mightier Than The Slingshot

ince the first choice for governor could not seem to follow instructions, Sam L. set about finding a replacement. As usual, God directed him to His choice. He told him to go see a farmer by the name of Jess, and one of his sons would be the new pick.

When Sam L. showed up, ol' man Jess called the boys to the house and paraded them in front of him. They were not a bad looking bunch of young men, but Sam L. did not have that my-hives-are-acting-up tingling feeling that he knew signaled God's validation. Maybe he had the wrong Mr. Jess. Maybe he had lost all feeling in his body. Maybe there was another son Mr. Jess had forgotten. When Sam L. asked if these were all the boys, Mr. Jess said he had one more, but he was just a young squirt, and they left him to finish milking the goats.

At Sam L.'s insistence, Mr. Jess sent one of the others to fetch the missing son. When David Ray came into the house, Sam L. started a fit of tingling so severe that it took Jess and all the boys to hold him still. When he finally calmed down, Sam L. took out the can of 10W-30 and poured it over David Ray's head. Not the most pleasant experience in the world but a small price to pay for getting to be governor. Of course it would be several years before David Ray took over the reins of government, so he went back to milking the goats, who, naturally, were laughing their horns off at this kid with motor oil for hair.

Meanwhile, back at the capital, Billy Sol just could not seem to shake his deep state of depression or the headache from that pickled pig's foot upside his head. Eventually, one of his aides suggested that some good music might cheer him up, and he just happened to know a young fellow who could pick a banjo better than a second grader can pick a nose. Not only did this boy know all of Charlie Daniels' stuff, but he could also play both parts to "Dueling Banjos" at the same time. Billy Sol told him to send for the musician. It couldn't make things any worse. (Wrong again, okra breath!)

You will never guess who the banjo picker turned out to be. Okay, so you made a lucky guess. When David Ray arrived at the Governor's Mansion, he was ushered straight in to see the main man himself. He was a little nervous but managed to get his banjo out and start picking a few old-time gospel numbers.

When he noticed that this did not seem to be cheering up the governor, he figured it was time to get a bit more lively. He started in on

"Dueling Banjos." Billy Sol's foot began to tap. Just one foot, but that's progress. Next he grabbed a fiddle and went straight on into "The Devil Came Down to Georgia." Can't nobody sit still on that one. By the middle of "Rocky Top," Billy Sol was dancing around the room like he had fire ants in his overalls. He had totally forgotten about how depressed he was. Everybody in the capitol thanked David Ray for what he had done and begged him to promise he would come back whenever the big guy got down.

Shortly thereafter another crisis reared its ugly head (which looked astonishingly like the famous coconut mentioned previously). It shook the very foundation on which the Alabama belief system was founded. If left unchecked, it could undermine this state's most cherished institution—SEC football. The football team from the neigh-

boring state of Georgia was laying waste to every other school in the conference. But this was not just any ordinary team. They had playing for them a giant named Herschel the Walker. On the field, he ran to and fro at will and scored points whenever he chose. The other teams were powerless to even slow him down, never mind stop him. The people were looking to Billy Sol for answers, but he was too old to go back to college. Besides, they had come up with that "no pass, no play" rule, and there was no way he could get past freshman chemistry.

During one of the games, Jess sent David Ray down to the stadium to see how his brothers were doing against this formidable opponent. When he got there, Coach Shug of the Jordan was hollering and screaming and threatening players with loss of scholarships, but no one would leave the safety of the bench. They would rather leave school than let Herschel run over them again.

David Ray knew that something must be done quickly, and it looked like *he* was going to have to be the one to do it. He systematically analyzed the play selection, blocking schemes, and cheerleaders of the opposing team. He determined that their game plan was to give the ball to the big guy and let him run over everybody. So far it was working to perfection. The chances of stopping him were a little less than the chance of inflicting serious bodily injury on a charging rhino with, say, a drinking straw.

Confidently, he walked up to Coach Shug and told him that he was not afraid to be put in the game. The coach was thrilled to have somebody, anybody—even this little shrimp—willing to go on the field. He started throwing shoulder

pads, hip pads, knee pads, and a helmet on the boy. When David Ray was able to crawl out from under this pile of stuff, he told the coach that he appreciated the offer, but that all that equipment severely hampered his efforts in such areas as seeing and breathing. All he needed were two pieces of paper, a pen, and a small box of crayons. Coach didn't really understand what was going on, but he was willing to try anything.

After writing on the paper for a few minutes, David Ray marched onto the field and right up to the Giant. After exchanging a few words, Herschel signed one of the pieces of paper, shook hands with David Ray, and ran out of the stadium. The other Bulldogs were so upset about his leaving that they went on to lose the game by forty points.

What David Ray had done was to explain to Herschel that due to a new school policy which combined course credits with rushing yardage, he had graduated during the first quarter. David Ray then handed him an authentic looking University of Georgia diploma: DEPLOMUH—u R a graduwait. The second piece of paper was an official-looking contract with one of the NFL's professional football teams. The contract included a signing bonus, plus allowed him to try out for the Olympic Bobsled Team. The strategy worked and it was a lot safer than slinging rocks at a fellow that big.

David Ray was a hero! He had returned SEC Football to its glory days. The players and fans carried him out of the stadium on their shoulders. They elected him Homecoming Queen, and they gave him the Key to the City and complimentary passes to the car wash so he could get that grease out of his hair. He was more popular than *Hee Haw* and *The Andy Griffith Show* combined.

After the celebration had ended, David Ray went back to his chores on Daddy's farm and his part-time job as banjo picker for the governor. But he could tell things were not the same between Billy Sol and him. It seemed that the governor was just a little jealous of David Ray's new celebrity status. David Ray's first clue was when he was pickin' and grinnin' one night during the governor's dinner, and Billy Sol's steak knife *accidentally* slipped and went flying about a quarter-inch above David Ray's left ear. His second clue was when he was pickin' and grinnin' the next night during the governor's dinner, and Billy Sol's steak knife *accidentally* slipped and went flying about a quarter-inch above David Ray's right ear.

David Ray thought that this might be a good time to take advantage of that Student Exchange Program with the Netherlands. But since he had no idea where or what the Netherlands were, maybe he could just hide out in the woods around south Alabama until things cooled off a bit. Hiding out was not going to be easy. He had the most famous and most popular face in the state. He even tried wearing glasses with a fake nose and mustache, but people still recognized him and would yell something like "How 'bout them Dawgs!" A dead giveaway.

In spite of a number of close encounters through the years, David Ray was able to run and hide until he finally had that one most important advantage over Billy Sol—he was still alive and Billy Sol was not. According to old Sam L. and a ratifying two-thirds vote of both houses, it was finally time for David Ray to ascend to the position of governor. So he did. Naturally, the first thing was a big inauguration party, which was pretty much the same as Billy Sol's (except with a lot less fried okra).

CHAPTER XVII

David Ray Meets Barbie Sue

avid Ray was determined to be a just and fair ruler to his people. He guided them into what would be years of peace and prosperity. He was a man of the people and spent many hours kissing babies, holding press conferences, and even served as master of ceremonies at the annual Fourth of July Phillystine Butt-Kickin' festivities. This was without question the most favorite celebration of the year and a good time was had by all—with the possible exception of the Phillystines.

Up until this time, God had been pleased with David Ray and even called him a man after His own heart. He had always followed His commands and tried to live a righteous life; however, it always seems that, no matter how well-intentioned, people are going to eventually mess up. David Ray knew the story about Billy Sol and the tangerines, but he wasn't worried about that happening to him—tangerines gave him an awful rash. But everyone has an Achilles' heel, and David Ray's turned out to be (get ready for a big surprise) . . . a woman. (Too bad he hadn't read the earlier chapter about Hoss. He would have been more aware of this potential problem.)

The way it happened, he was down at Gulf Shores for a few days of vacation from the rigors of office. He was sipping on a frozen butter-bean daiquiri on the condo balcony and looking for fishing boats on the horizon, when his eyes momentarily glanced down toward the beach. There he spied a young lady lying on a towel and wearing about the most nothing bikini he had ever seen. And in all the places where the bikini was nothing, she was something.

Wouldn't nothing do but for him to get a little better acquainted. She was, after all, one of his constituents, and he thought she might have some good ideas on how to reform the Social Security System (ain't nobody buying *that*, Dave). He hollered out and asked what her sign was, where she was from, and would she like to meet the fellow that got rid of Herschel the Walker. She couldn't hear him very well over the roar of the waves and thought he said something like "sign your form and follow her shell to the water." She chalked it up mostly to the daiquiri, waved politely, and went back to her tanning.

David Ray was not going to be so easily brushed off. He quickly summoned one of his highway patrol bodyguards and sent him down to tell the young woman what he had said. Also, his messenger was to ask her if she would like to have a daiquiri, to have dinner with a hero, and time permitting, to bear several of the governor's children. David Ray watched anxiously from the balcony as the messenger approached the sunbather. He grew even more tense as the patrolman approached the wrong woman. The one to whom he was talking looked something like the mutant offspring of a liaison between an ugly mule and Shamu. Through a series of loud whistles and hand gestures, David Ray was finally able to steer him back to the intended target.

Come to find out, the young lady's name was Barbie Sue, and as a matter of fact, after lying out in that hot sun, she wouldn't mind having a drink with the governor. The patrolman escorted her back to the condo and introduced her to David Ray. The lawman was promptly dismissed to go give out some parking tickets. The Guv and his new friend

got to talking and drinking daiquiris, and the alcohol started affecting certain portions of their memory, like the fact that they were both currently married—to *other* folks. As will sometimes happen in these situations (99.76 percent of the time, according to soap opera plots), they soon crossed over the line and violated the seventh and tenth commandments. Suffering from severe hangovers and a ton of guilt, they said their good-byes the next morning, and she stumbled out the door, and as far as they knew, out of each other's lives. (Not likely!)

Not long afterward, David Ray got an overnight, express mail, return-receipt requested letter from Barbie Sue. She thanked him for a lovely evening, hoped that he was doing well, and mentioned that she was pregnant—by him. David Ray wrote back that she was welcome, he was doing fine, and that maybe it would be best if she just gave her husband credit for her current condition. Then he was informed that her husband had been gone for several months and there was no way that would work. David Ray knew that as soon as this got in the tabloids, his days as governor were numbered. He had to do the right thing and marry Barbie Sue. But first, he had to do the wrong thing and get rid of her current husband.

Her husband, Capt. Hugh Riah, was stationed at nearby Pensacola Naval Air Station and was out to sea on training exercises. The military had already discovered the importance of air superiority even though at this time there was no such thing as an actual airplane. This technical-ity was overcome by using a primitive catapult device consisting of a hickory sapling, which when bent nearly double and released could fling a man several hundred feet into the air. As he reached the peak of the ascent, he would look around for enemy ships or schools of marlin and scream out their location just prior to plunging back into the ocean at around 120 miles per hour.

These men were the forerunners of the modern day aircraft carrier pilots and were known as "idiots." Capt. Hugh Riah was an idiot. Not enough of one to believe that he could father a child from several hundred miles away but still enough of one to be shot up into the air like a human spitball. Due to the rather unpredictable nature of hickory saplings and the wind, it was not unusual for a number of idiots to be lost during war exercises. David Ray got word to the admiral that if *perchance* Hugh Riah happened to be one of the unfortunate ones that got run over by the boat, or slammed headfirst back into the deck instead of the water, or was eaten by a large fish, it would be a feather in the Admiral's cap. The admiral was crazy about feathers, so sure enough, the poor captain just happened to "accidentally" meet with an untimely (around 9:34 A.M.) demise.

Capt. Hugh Riah was posthumously awarded the Distinguished Idiot Slinging Cross and buried somewhere at sea, which is where he already was, they think. The admiral got a bushel of feathers, so he was really tickled. Barbie Sue, as the devastated widow, mourned for several hours prior to a lavish wedding in the governor's mansion and the birth of their son.

David Ray had apparently gotten away with this whole series of dirty deeds, and his popularity as governor had never been higher. *Apparently* being the key word here. Getting rid of Hugh Riah, even at someone else's hand, had added the sixth commandment to his list of transgressions. He would not be smiling for long.

An old preacher by the name of Nat dropped by the governor's office one day with a message. "God don't like ugly, and what you did was ugly!" Nat was a little hard of hearing and assumed everybody else was also. David Ray got the message not only loud, but clear. He may have pulled the wool over a lot of eyes, but there just wasn't enough wool on the planet to fool God. David Ray knew he was in deep trouble. Nat went on to say that the rest of David Ray's life would be one crisis after another. His people would be constantly at war with all kinds of folks. His

young 'uns would all be royal pains, even to the point of taking away his governorship and running him off. There was a high price to pay for the combination of daiquiris and a bikini.

As old Nat had predicted, the years after that were hard and took their toll on David Ray. He would spend the rest of his life regretting the consequences of a few minutes of pleasure. Finally he reached the age when he could no longer gov-

ern, and it was time to pick a successor. Over the years, he had had a number of wives and a bunch of children. He picked his favorite son, Sonny, to carry on the family line as Governor of Alabama. This practice of passing the public office around in the same family is still popular today, not only in Alabama but also in numerous other states. This practice may have been instituted by the Massachutians before they were run out of Alabama. They do seem to have one particular family with a compound in Hyannis Port who has maintained a position of political dominance for years.

Sonny began his first term as governor with all the high ideals of his father. He wanted to be a good and fair leader who inspired his people to greatness. In his prayers, instead of material wealth or great power, he asked God for wisdom. This pleased God to the point that He told Sonny that He would not only give him wisdom but also the other things that he didn't ask for. Anybody smart enough to ask for wisdom is already a pretty smart fellow.

Not long after he assumed office, his wisdom was put to the test. Two women, both of whom claimed to have given birth to the same child, came before him to settle the dispute. Sonny pondered for only a moment and then called for one of his guards. He instructed the soldier to take out his sword, cut the baby in half, and give each woman a half. One of the women immediately started screaming not to harm the child but to give it to the other woman. Sonny knew that this was the child's rightful mother and gave her the child.

The people were amazed at the depth of Sonny's wisdom. He could program a VCR without help from his children and could solve the puzzles on *Wheel of Fortune* without buying a single vowel. He came up with many wise proverbs, such as "A penny saved is a penny earned," and "A stitch in time saves you from putting all your eggs in a barrel with spoiled apples." (Some years later, these were erroneously attributed to some poor fellow named Richard Almanac.)

God honored His promise and soon Sonny had wealth beyond all imagination. He built many new buildings, entire cities, and even built a magnificent temple to honor God. Besides that, the boy was constantly writing poems and songs and was just a bundle of talent. He made treaties with other states that ensured peace and added to his wealth through trade agreements. But in order to get some of these treaties, it was necessary for Sonny to marry daughters of other governors. Soon he found himself with so many wives that it was impossible to find an empty bathroom except in the middle of the night. And even then he could hardly find his way to the john with all the pantyhose hanging from the shower rod.

This was one of the little things about which God had warned Sonny. Don't be marrying no women from other states, especially states above the Mason-Dixon Line. As smart as Sonny was, he, like a number of his predecessors and successors, got in trouble over women.

This disobedience resulted not only in his being defeated for governor during the next election, but also none of his sons were ever elected to follow in his footsteps.

God was upset. This governor thing that the people just had to have was not working out. Billy Sol, David Ray, and now Sonny had all been disobedient and had all gotten themselves and the state in a mess.

God decided, once again, that He was through talking to these governors because, sooner or later, they always let Him down. The Chosen People were just going to have to do things the hard way for a while.

CHAPTER XVIII

This Must Be The End Because I Can't Think Of Anything Else

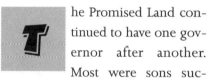he Promised Land continued to have one governor after another. Most were sons succeeding fathers. Some were wives succeeding husbands. And even though God had chosen not to speak to any of these future governors, He still continued to send guidance and help for the people through men known as prophets.

These ol' boys were usually viewed as nuts and kooks, but invariably, whatever they told the people came true. When the people did listen and tried to do good, things worked out well, and when they didn't, things were rough. Fortunately, there were enough good people and good deeds that God continued to bless and prosper them. They were, after all, His Chosen People, and no matter how disappointed He might be over their disobedience, they were still His.

Many of the prophecies dealt with things that would someday become intertwined with the very essence of being a Redneck. One of these prophecies foretold the single most important advancement in the history of Rednecking—the invention of the pickup truck. Properly equipped with a gun rack, tool box, good dog standing proud in the back, and good woman sitting close in the front, the pickup became a living extension of the Redneck man. Later on, when four-wheel drive and those big tires were added, the space shuttle paled in comparison.

Most of the other prophecies related to what most non-Rednecks might consider leisure pursuits, but to a serious Redneck, they were and are as vital as air. No self-respecting Redneck can ride around in a big ol' pickup like that with a little sissy canoe hanging out the back. He has to have a bass boat. Since no one has accurately measured the top speed

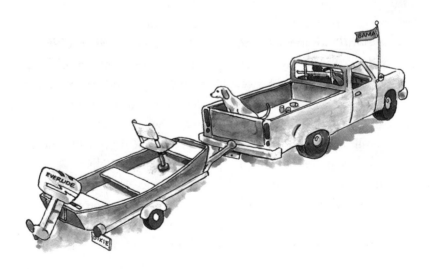

of a largemouth, this boat must be capable of speeds just short of lightning. This, of course, requires at least a 250-horsepower outboard motor, which keeps the boat mostly in the air so that it touches the water only every hundred yards or so. Flying up and down the river at full throttle is about as close to Heaven as earth-bound mortals can come. If you accidentally catch a few fish, all the better.

Another prophecy predicted what would become, without question, one of the most hallowed times of the year—deer season. For months prior to its beginning, the Redneck must gather, sort, clean, and arrange the sacred equipment—rifles, bows and arrows, tree stands, and assorted aromas to conceal and attract. He may very well wear camouflage clothes, hats, and boots year round. When the season officially opens, nothing can keep him from his destiny in the woods. In terms of priority, this event far exceeds such other ordinary occasions as wedding anniversaries, children's birthdays, children's births, funerals, weddings, personal major surgery, and world wars. And in the woods he will most likely remain until officially notified by a credible authority that the season is, in fact, over. When he is dragged, kicking and screaming, back to civilization, it may very well be necessary to resort to some form of a primitive purification ritual to aid the hunter in returning to a normal human existence where he will languish until it is once again time to search for the elusive buck.

There are some other pursuits that can be acknowledged as leisure but that in no way diminishes their importance. These activities not only provide a needed diversion from the rigors of daily life but are also the source of most of the Redneck heroes and role models.

Any Saturday night, you will find a goodly portion of the Redneck population glued to the TV, or the more fortunate will be down at the coliseum, where they are deeply involved in helping their favorite good-guy rassler whup the bad feller. Say what you want, but it don't get any more real than that. And if there is a NASCAR event within a couple hundred miles, somebody needs to get on down there and see if Richard Petty can't pull out that old magic just one more time.

These are only a few of the things that distinguish the Chosen People from other mere mortals. Inbred in every Redneck, although not always evident, is an extremely strong sense of God, family, and country. A Redneck will help you any way he can, and if he can't, he probably knows somebody who can. If he likes you, he'll give you the shirt off his back. If he don't like you, he just might knock the shirt off yours. But you won't have to wonder long which it will be. He'll let you know pretty quick and in plain language.

As the years have passed, the Chosen People have even learned to live in relative harmony alongside the once-hated Yankee. Some have even moved north and dwelt among them, and train loads of them have moved south. Once here, they are harder to get rid of than fleas on a long-haired black dog.

Rednecks in varying forms and degrees can now be found all over this great land of ours. Some are purebred and couldn't change if they wanted to (which they most likely don't). Others may be well-educated, sophisticated professionals.